A Joy-Filled Amazement

TONY ANTHONY

MW

Montgomery Wood Publishing
P.O. Box 56 Ukiah, CA 95482

Library of Congress Cataloging-in-Publication Data

Anthony, Tony, A Joy-Filled Amazement.

ISBN: 978-0-578-35722-5

1.Spiritual Life 2.Anthony, Tony

A Joy-Filled Amazement

Below Sea Level

*T*here comes a time in the life of the lucky ones—I am fortunate to be among them— when life becomes so unbearable it breaks open and allows us to peer below the surface and glimpse something deeper. It happened for me when I was twenty-three and found myself lost.

It's when Maharishi found me.

It was the Spring of 1970 and I was a homeless Vietnam Vet sleeping below sea level in the hold of a decommissioned anchovy boat in Santa Barbara Harbor. The previous autumn, I had returned home from my tour in Vietnam serving as a combat correspondent in an infantry unit. I had spent a year photographing and reporting on combat engagements—firefights, ambushes, villages burned, North Vietnamese and Vietcong soldiers taken prisoner, Americans mired in a guerrilla war—things, one would think, a human need not bear witness to. The war changed me. It also raised deep questions I couldn't find answers to. I had been traumatized and knew it. I had no clue how to deal with it.

I returned home to my family in Connecticut for a few weeks and then moved to Boston where I shared an apartment with an old prep-school roommate, David Rottenberg. We were kindred spirits and had been co-editors of the Jabberwocky, the school newspaper. An excellent writer, he went on to graduate from Columbia and published his first novel while I was fighting in Vietnam. We became sounding boards for each other in our quest for finding answers to life's deepest questions. We opened our apartment to assorted hippies along with the mind-expanding drugs they brought with them. I dropped acid, which opened my eyes enough to let me know I didn't want any more of the cold and damp of the Northeast. So, David and I headed across country to California in his '65 white Mustang convertible in search of bliss. California was the place to be; it was where everyone smoked pot and hippie chicks offered free love, and some even found a guru. In Los Angeles, David and I stopped in at Paramahansa Yogananda's Self Realization Fellowship in Malibu. We chanced upon a young monk who explained what it took to become an acolyte. It involved a one-year trial period of study and meditation just to get started. Spiritual hunger had been an undercurrent of my life since I was a child, but I knew this was not the place or time; it was too cloistered, too intense. What I needed now was just the opposite.

A week later, David and I parted at the Pacific Coast Highway and I set out hitch-hiking to visit my sister in San Francisco. As fate would have it, my ride dropped me in Santa Barbara. Captured by the sparkling water of the Pacific Ocean, I wandered down to the marina and met a fellow working on a dilapidated old wooden anchovy boat. His name was John and he commiserated with me about how much work it would take to make it seaworthy and offered me a place to sleep in the boat's empty hold, if I was willing to help with repairs.

Due to the inertia brought on by the daily use of marijuana, the work never progressed very far. I couldn't continue to work for no pay, but I didn't want to leave the laidback marina lifestyle either, so I found a job selling baitfish to the fishing fleet. I earned $10 per day cash, which, given my free lodging on the boat, was barely enough to keep me fed and supplied with weed. I enjoyed life among the colorful group of outliers who lived in the marina. They drank every night, smoked pot and were into various hallucinogenic drugs like mescaline and peyote. Because Vietnam had left me a mess, it was a perfect fit.

My life was more of an experiment in staying alive than actually living. I didn't realize it at the time, but I had replaced the bizarre unreality of Vietnam with the unreal haze of hallucinogens. Santa Barbara was the perfect place for me. It was home to the University of California and several smaller colleges, and had become the epicenter of the nationwide social upheaval of disenfranchised youth at war with "the establishment" and "the military-industrial complex." The revolution was giving birth to a new way of thinking. The Vietnam War had shaken America to the core, creating a kind of spiritual void, especially for the young. Meanwhile, marijuana and hallucinogenic drugs had opened the door to higher consciousness, which at least temporarily, filled the void. Unfortunately, many burned out on drugs and never got to step through the door. My old persona as "a preppy kid from suburban Connecticut" had been blown apart in Vietnam. My nerves were shot, I had a permanent tremor in my hands and a hyper-thyroid from the stress of combat. My head was filled with constant noise and images that became unbearable when I closed my eyes at night. What I didn't know is that I suffered from PTSD before it had a name.

My savior arrived in the guise of an old Dutchman. One night, while sitting on the carpet in the wheelhouse with Captain John serenading his girlfriend on the guitar, we heard a rap on the door. I opened it and was met by a man with white hair tumbling out from under a black, peaked seaman's cap. There were horizontal wrinkles on his forehead and penetrating blue eyes beneath his eyebrows. But his beard, snow white and precisely trimmed, gave him the air of a distinguished gentleman. His smile was radiant as he stepped in with well-worn boots and a cane. Hans Sebbelov was a longtime friend of John's who had mysteriously gone missing for six months. John, of course, was eager to know where he had been. With the help of his cane, Hans lowered himself onto the carpet, and began to recount an amazing tale. After receiving a fatal diagnosis from an incurable disease, his doctor suggested that his only hope might be a holy man in India. John had heard about Maharishi Mahesh Yogi, who had gained worldwide notoriety when the Beatles sought him out in search of spiritual enlightenment in 1968. Hans bought a ticket to India, showed up at Maharishi's ashram in Rishikesh at the foot of the Himalayas, and stayed for half a year. He told us that Maharishi taught him techniques that allowed him to travel inside his body to heal his organs. His descriptions were vivid, and utterly believable. I was so enthralled by his account, that I wanted to hear more. I needed to hear more. So, he invited me to join him for a walk around the harbor.

It was a blustery evening with waves crashing against the seawall and wind whipping steel halyards against the aluminum masts on the sailboats. Nature's wrath was a fitting soundtrack for a conversation that steered toward the subject of war. I mentioned that I had recently returned from Vietnam, but Hans seemed to know that already. Without letting on, he seemed to know a lot about me. He said he understood the trauma of war from his own experience in combat in World War II. When I said I felt lucky to have survived my combat tour in Vietnam uninjured, he paused, turned his sparkling eyes directly at mine and said, "The worst wounds are those that affect the mind." I felt like he had taken an x-ray of my brain. Still walking, we reached the end of the jetty just when a giant wave crashed against the rocks and sent a huge arc of spray over us. Yet, the two of us stood there completely dry. I had the inexplicable feeling that we were being shielded by an invisible cosmic umbrella.

In the coming years, this was not the only time I would find myself protected by this umbrella.

We rode in Hans' Volkswagen Beetle to Denny's where our far-reaching conversation lasted well into the night. I was astounded by his ability to answer some of my deepest questions about life and war. He spoke about what he called "shell shock,"

11

what is now called Post-Traumatic Stress Disorder (PTSD), and explained how traumas like those experienced in combat are stored in the body as stresses that affect our health and well-being. He told me that the most important technique he learned from Maharishi was Transcendental Meditation. This meditation, he said, allowed the body such a deep level of rest that even profound stress could be released.

It was late when Hans dropped me back at the marina. He pulled his VW up to the curb and shut off the engine. With a smile on his bearded face, he peered into my eyes and said, "I'm going to give you four important rules that will change your life for the better." At that moment, Hans was no longer the one speaking. He had disappeared. Maharishi Mahesh Yogi was sitting beside me. I recognized his face from posters I had seen advertising TM: His thick black hair, parting on one side, draping over his shoulders. His graying beard resting below his chin. His curved cheek bones filling out the gentleness of his appearance. I stared in amazement. I had never met Maharishi but, nonetheless, he was completely familiar. It felt as if I'd never not known him.

"First and most important," he said, "you must begin Transcendental Meditation. There is a TM center in Los Angeles. Go there and ask for Jerry Jarvis. Make certain Jerry is the one to teach you.

"Second, you must get a simple job, like driving a truck.

"Third, rent an apartment where you can live alone and in peace.

"And fourth," he giggled, "give up women."

This last point hit its mark. I was holding onto a dead-end relationship with an Australian journalist I had met in Vietnam.

Had I mentioned Kate to Hans? I didn't think so. But obviously Maharishi knew.

Sitting next to Maharishi in the front seat of a Volkswagen was beyond anything I had experienced in this earthly reality. He was as real to me as my own hand and I felt the full comfort and joy of his presence.

The Greatest Relief

Swept up in this moment of euphoria, I immediately made plans to follow my new path. I called David, who now lived on Santa Monica Beach in Los Angeles. He said he was happy to have me stay with him and told me he had just started TM himself. A day later he dropped me off at the Transcendental Center in L.A. barely in time for the 7:30 Preparatory Lecture. Stepping through the door, I felt as if I had found a refuge from the crazy world outside. The silence was palpable. A luminous young woman ushered me into a packed lecture hall and showed me to the only available seat—on the floor in front of a low stage.

The speaker was a fellow only slightly older than myself, but who looked quite a bit more together. In contrast to my long hair, scruffy beard, and ratty clothes, he had a stylish haircut and wore a sport jacket, a pressed shirt, and a tie. He introduced himself as Kenny Edwards and spoke in a soft, confident manner, recapping the previous week's lecture in which he had explained the benefits of Transcendental Meditation. Tonight's talk was meant to prepare those hoping to learn, with details about how TM worked. He explained the use of a mantra—a meaningless sound with a profound effect. By repeating the mantra, he said, the mind automatically settles down to finer levels of thought. The deepest rest comes when the mind, where the distractions and worries of everyday life reside, *transcends* the thinking level. This *transcendence* is to a deeper level, an infinite field of *absolute Pure Being*, the essence of life. This, he explained, is the core of Transcendental Meditation.

I didn't need convincing. After my experience of being with Maharishi in Santa Barbara, I didn't feel that I needed to know the particulars. It was enough that the guru who brought the technique to the Western World had strongly suggested I do it. I was more than ready. Kenny ended the lecture with a caveat. He told us that people who had used non-prescription drugs, including marijuana in the last two weeks, would have to wait for a month before they learned to meditate.

I thought that might pertain to others, but not to me. After all, I had my orders from a higher authority.

I waited in line with other participants to sign up to be initiated on the coming Saturday, two days hence. When I returned a warm smile to the woman sitting behind the desk, and requested Jerry Jarvis to teach me, she told me while hiding a sweet smirk that wouldn't be possible. Jerry was the National Chairman. Besides, he was out of town.

I didn't press the issue by mentioning who it was that had instructed me to ask.

Saturday, a glittering sun was shining on the buildings as I took the bus up Wilshire Boulevard to Westwood Village. All was right with the world. For the ceremony, I had the thirty-five-dollar fee in my pocket and the required basket of fruit and flowers in my lap. I felt blissful already and I hadn't even learned to meditate. The staff at the TM center on Gayley Avenue welcomed the new soon-to-be initiates with elated smiles. The TM people appeared more to float than walk. They smiled as if they had recently arrived from another planet where everyone lived in perpetual happiness. They all spoke in muted voices similar to Kenny's, which imbued their words with an otherworldly, protective power that seemed to sweep away any obstacle in their path. I was reminded of the wave that had arched above Hans and me in Santa Barbara.

The contrast between them and myself made me painfully aware that part of me was still stuck back in Vietnam. A few months wasn't enough time to process a year of war. My head was doing its best just to catch up with being back in the normal world. Now I was about to begin a spiritual practice I wasn't sure I was fully prepared for. On the other hand, I was so hungry for relief I knew I needed to dive right in.

It was no exaggeration to say the TM people were genuinely loving and kind. The mission of Maharishi's movement is to make the world a better place by creating peace in the hearts of people, one person at a time. There was so much goodness and light in the TM center, and I was so eager to be part of it, that I stopped questioning anything.

A woman floated toward me, beneath her invisible umbrella of bliss. Eyeing the basket in my hands and smiling disarmingly, she made a statement that sounded more like a question, a form of speech I was to become used to hearing in the coming years.

"So, you're here for initiation?" she said, and led me down a corridor where the silence was as deep as a temple. She left me in front of a door holding my fruit and flowers.

Before slipping away, she whispered sweetly, "You will take off your shoes?" and left me with a dose of her joy.

A minute later, the door opened to reveal Kenny Edwards in a fresh pressed shirt and tie. On his face was the same kind of blissful smile. He plucked the form I had filled out the night of the lecture from the basket, and we took seats in the small room in front of a table covered with a white tablecloth. While he reviewed the details on my form, I studied the table that was set up as an altar with sparkling brass implements. One held a lit candle and another a burning stick of incense. There was a small bowl with rice, one filled with water, and another with fragrant tan powder. A small chunk of camphor sat in something that looked like a genie's lamp. Behind them, leaning against the wall, a painted portrait of a dignified bearded monk captured my attention. He was clothed in an orange robe with his forehead painted orange as well. He sat, cross-legged with his back perfectly straight with a powerful gaze in his eyes. The compelling man in the picture completely erased any lingering doubts and encouraged me to accept whatever was to come. Just seeing him put me completely at ease and I let go of any fear that the impending journey would be too much to handle.

I attributed the vibrant energy in the room to Kenny who had mentioned in his lecture that he'd recently returned from teacher training with Maharishi in Rishikesh, India. He stood up in front of the altar and motioned me to stand beside him. He explained he was about to perform a ceremony called a *puja* to honor Maharishi's teacher, Guru Dev, the monk in the picture from whom the meditation came. He sang some verses in Sanskrit while circling the flowers, the incense, the candle, and the burning camphor in front of the portrait. Then he made an offering of the fruit, sprinkling them with water, and the flowers.

When he finished, we knelt together in front of the picture until he motioned me into a chair, sat down beside me and softly repeated my mantra. He gave me instructions to repeat it more softly and then, finally, silently. There were a few simple instructions about how to meditate before he told me to close my eyes and continue.

Then I meditated for the first time.

I have no idea how long I meditated. It may have been for a few seconds or for an eternity; time didn't seem to exist. When I heard Kenny's voice telling me to open my eyes, I had just experienced the greatest relief I had ever known. As unbelievable as it may sound, *ever* also included my past lifetimes. I can't say how I knew this; I just did.

Kenny asked, "It was easy?"

I had to think. "Actually, I don't remember anything."

He flashed me the blissful meditator's smile I had seen on several faces.

I added another thought. "It was like it never happened."

"That's called transcending."

After that, he told me to meditate for ten minutes. "I'll be back," he said and left the room. After settling in, I felt Maharishi sit down beside me. Part of me wanted to open my eyes to see if he was truly there. The other part told me not to. So, I didn't. Afterwards, I wanted to ask Kenny if Maharishi would always be meditating with me, but he was nowhere to be found. I knew that if Maharishi came to me again, I would have my answer. And if he didn't, that would be okay too; he had already given me the greatest gift I'd ever received, the gift of transcending.

A Glimpse of the Divine

*O*utside on the sidewalk beside Gayley Avenue, I walked into a bright, sparkling world imbued with a soft blissfulness. My crystal-clear vision made all the colors around me animated and vibrant. Cars were so shiny and vivid they looked like storybook toys just driven from the factory. Their paint was so deep and saturated that I felt as if I could sink my fingers into it. The people walking by were over-the-top beautiful. Trees were statuesque. Buildings were like architectural models, more unreal than real, yet striking. *Everything* was beautiful. Everything I passed was alive with cosmic energy. I had no idea how my world could have changed so dramatically after just a single meditation, yet the proof was right in front of me. I had been transformed. I was clear, transparent, as if life was happening through me—as if I were the world, and the world was me. I was not only part of it, I *was* it. The things around me seemed as familiar as my childhood bedroom, comfortable and non-threatening. Maybe I was letting go of the fear of being killed by unseen enemies. Nothing on the street appeared to be booby-trapped or about to explode.

For the first time in a long time, I felt *safe*.

I was surrounded by a deep silence out of which came the sound of sweet birds chirping. I felt like I had been dipped into a pool of honey. Only, the honey was bliss. This was the truth of how life could be—and really is—if we can just appreciate it. It was so simple, so pure, so clear, so real and "right-in-front-of-me" that I was finally able to see it. It had been here all along, but I had always looked past it. Now, for once, I was appreciating the joy of existence. Everything, including myself, was contained within it—right here in Westwood Village, California. I had been waiting lifetimes for this relief. A single meditation had allowed me to sink beneath my complicated thinking mind, into a warm and bottomless ocean of bliss. I felt a smile appear on my face. And reflected in a shop window I saw, from the outside, what that looked like.

Afterwards, still in a kind of dream state, I rode the bus back to David's place in Santa Monica. We did our evening meditation together and made it a routine in the days to come. Meditation had created a bond between us and a desire for me to be around meditators. David invited me to stay as long as I paid a share of the rent. I was fortunate to find a job doing deliveries for Campbell's Bookstore in Westwood Village, a few blocks from the TM center, where the work was practically stress free. I spent most of the day driving around Beverly Hills dropping off books at the homes of movie stars. Since I began to meditate, I was happier. I had less anxiety and was more willing to take things as they came. I recognized TM was what had been missing from my life and felt eternally grateful to Hans and Maharishi for introducing me to it.

A few days following my initiation, I returned to the TM Center to make sure I was meditating properly. After my checking session, I saw Kenny in the lobby chatting with a jovial red-headed gentleman I recognized was Jerry Jarvis. Eavesdropping on their conversation, I heard Jerry mention that "the boss" was coming to California. He was, of course, referring to Maharishi, who, I found out later, was coming to give a one-month advanced course at Humboldt College in Arcata. The thought of seeing Maharishi in person thrilled me. I decided then and there to go to Arcata which was a few day's drive north of Santa Monica. Excited that I now had a mission, I thought things would unfold quickly. My job at Campbell's Bookstore would provide the money to buy a van to camp in and make my escape from L.A. possible. I thought my clear mind and the power of my intention would make anything possible.

But first, as someone told me later, I still had some old karma to work off.

Wanted for Murder

After work one evening, after the bus dropped me at the end of Wilshire, I crossed the pedestrian bridge to the beach parking lot and walked right into the perfect vehicle for my escape to see Maharishi at Humboldt College. A well-worn Volkswagen van, orange with a white roof, had a "for sale" sign taped in a window. The price was $400, the exact amount I had saved, so I called the phone number on the sign, which turned out to belong to a young man living in a front room in our apartment house. I met with him briefly and closed the deal. I could hardly believe that only a few months before I had been in the depths of despair and now my dreams were coming true. I owned a vehicle that would take me where I wanted. Within days, I had built a platform in the back for a bed, bought a futon, a Coleman gas stove, and a jerry can for water. I was now able to camp on the way to Humboldt, about six hundred miles north. It would take only a few weeks of work before I had the money for food and gas. I could already smell the clean, pine-scented air and taste the water in clear mountain streams.

Two L.A. police detectives were not part of that dream.

One morning, at the bookstore, I found the two men waiting for me. They flashed their badges, introduced themselves and gave me this news: The young man I had bought the van from had been found murdered. I was a suspect, they wanted to question me. They had already visited our apartment house and interviewed David, who, when asked, told them that I had purchased the van, which in the eyes of the detectives, tied me to the crime. They had found $400 cash in the victim's pocket, which was the amount I had paid. The detectives also had done a little research and knew I had recently returned from Vietnam, which the detectives found of great interest.

I agreed to let them drive me downtown to the Los Angeles Police Station, where they fingerprinted me and interrogated me in a room with a two-sided mirror along one wall. They used the "good cop/bad cop" routine to question me with the bad cop eyeing me menacingly.

I could hardly believe it when one said, "You were a sergeant in the army, right? Sergeants carry .45 automatics, right? Our victim was killed with a .45 automatic. So why don't you save us all a lot of trouble and confess?" I thought, did I really here him saying that? Am I a character in a movie? The whole episode would've been funny had the potential consequences not been so dire.

26

I had been in the infantry so, of course, I was trained to use guns. Their potential case against me hinged on my being a soldier. I told the detectives that although the victim had lived in the same house, I had only met him once, when I bought the van. But that didn't deter them because it seemed I was the best lead they had. To make matters worse, Charles Manson was in the news at that time, so with my long hair and beard, I looked the part of a killer in the eyes of any L.A. detective. I felt like I was acting in a cheap television drama. The problem was, the show was playing out in real life.

After my interrogation, one of the detectives dropped me back at work and ordered me not to leave town, which I wanted to, now more than ever. The next day, a plain clothes policeman hiding behind a newspaper, was waiting for me at the bus stop and rode with me to work. A different cop followed me home in the evening. This went on for days. They were also following David. The police thought we might have been drug dealers and in on the crime together, so we both agreed to a polygraph test and passed, but still, no exoneration, no relief. Finally, a week later, the police solved another murder and tied the killer to this crime.

I was sure that my recent experience with meditation helped me through the ordeal. For the most part, I watched it unfold as if the events were separate from me. It wasn't that the situation didn't upset me; it did. But the drama seemed to develop outside me rather than within. If this ordeal was a case of working off bad karma, the results were promising. Many positive things were happening since I had begun to meditate and my desires were being fulfilled quickly. A traveling companion for my trip to Humboldt appeared effortlessly. David was eager to introduce me to a young woman he had recently met and was consumed with. His description of her was completely enchanting. Gloria was beautiful, of course, and exotic. She was half-Japanese, half-Jewish, wrote poetry, painted watercolors and, as he put it, was almost always nearly naked. I fell in love with her before I even saw her. I met Gloria when David brought me along to a party at the apartment she shared with an Englishman who was a drug dealer to the stars. Gloria moved around the crowded room with the grace of a dancer serving herb tea, giggling as she went. She was, as David promised, nearly naked. She was five-feet two and thin. Her skin was colored amber from the sun and her hair was a light shade of mahogany.

David, Gloria and I quickly became a threesome. She was mostly David's friend but there was a subtle attraction between us percolating beneath the surface. We all hung together most nights and spent weekends on the beach or hiking in the Malibu hills. One night after dinner with a group of friends in a restaurant in Topanga Canyon, I stood up to take a walk alone.

"Can I come?" Gloria asked softly.

When she took my hand and followed me outside without asking David to join us, everyone recognized the shift in her allegiance. She was letting him know she had chosen me. I have to admit, I had some residual guilt but in these type of situations women do the choosing and walking out with Gloria felt so sweet, just another scene in the movie script being written by a cosmic screenwriter. Gloria and I left the restaurant with our hearts pounding. We walked hand-in-hand up the dark canyon road leading into the great unknown. At the top of a hill, we turned down a dirt road that dropped us into a meadow where we sat back-to-back in the tall grass and talked.

I never told Gloria about my desire to have a traveling companion so I was overwhelmed when she said, "A few nights ago I dreamt you were leaving and I was with you."

I wondered if she was really saying what I thought she was. But I took the leap, invited her to come along with me, and held my breath waiting for an answer.

She replied by asking, "Do you really mean it?"

I said, "You dreamed it, didn't you?"

We turned to kiss, my first since returning from Vietnam, and I was thrilled by the feeling of her soft lips. When we made love, I felt like I had taken flight, leaving the harshness of war on the ground as I soared through layers of soft cotton clouds.

A week later, Gloria and I bought a puppy, named him Thoreau, and escaped from L.A. in my Volkswagen van.

Being a Hippie

We were the perfect hippie couple. Gloria was a kind and gentle person who had a wonderful influence on me. Her outlook on life was simple, healthy and practical. She followed a strict vegan diet and cooked only organic food, mostly brown rice and steamed vegetables. I quit smoking and drinking and became a vegetarian. This was quite an about-face from the Army meat-and-potatoes diet and my subsequent fast-food binge. Whenever we stopped to camp for the night, I sat on the bed in the back of the van and meditated. We were happy together and excited to be heading into uncharted territory. We drove up Mount Whitney and camped beneath a grove of pine trees beside a crystal-clear stream with a snow-capped peak looming protectively above us. Reveling in the serenity of the surroundings, I disobeyed my initiator's instructions and began meditating for longer than the prescribed twenty minutes. I found it easy to disregard rules and consequences living in such innocent pleasure. Even though I believed I would do anything to be part of Maharishi's teaching, I disobeyed his most basic instruction without a second thought. Lulled by the seductiveness of this life, my goal to reach Humboldt for his lecture moved to the back of my mind.

We stayed until we ran out of food, headed down the mountain to restock our supplies in a place called Lone Pine, and then drove north into Inyo National Forest. After that, we visited crowded Yosemite National Park where our small bus was sandwiched between two giant RV's. Still, we enjoyed the immense beauty of the park, and swam in the freezing cold water of the Tuolumne River. Thoreau chased squirrels and swam with us in the lakes and streams. Gloria cooked meals on the camping stove, played her guitar and sang. I meditated and wrote an endless stream of poems, mostly about Vietnam, hoping to purge myself of the demons of war. We had no responsibilities beyond feeding ourselves and Thoreau. Neither Gloria nor I needed to be anywhere other than where we were. It was about as stress-free an existence as I could imagine. My hair had grown over my shoulders and my beard filled out as much as it was going to. Everywhere we went we met hippies like ourselves and talked about the great relief of being free of most earthly constraints.

We were living in the moment. Wasn't that the Buddhist ideal? "The secret of health for both mind and body is not to mourn for the past, not to worry about the future, or not to anticipate troubles, but to live in the present moment wisely and earnestly." Yes, but as I was about to learn, that doesn't mean you can move forward oblivious to the future.

Seeing Maharishi

When Gloria and I left Santa Monica, the only plan had been to get to Arcata where Maharishi was holding an advanced meditation course. And the closer we came to Arcata, the stronger my desire to see him became. When we crossed the Golden Gate Bridge and were into the rolling hills of northern California, I was feeling drawn to Humboldt State like metal to a magnet. Gloria was less keen to see Maharishi than I, but she viewed my obsession as a part of our adventure and was happy enough to go along. We arrived at the college in the afternoon and some friendly students steered us to a grove of redwoods behind the campus. It turned out that the forest housed a small village of campers who had come to see Maharishi, but, like us, hadn't officially applied for the course. While I was living an idyllic life on the road, practicalities had escaped me. Course requirements, registration, cost, had never occurred to me. If my goal was to hear Maharishi speak, I had lost sight of the means to make that happen. Enrollment was full. We would not be taking the course.

Even so, we learned the times when Maharishi's lectures were to be held in the gymnasium and Gloria and I joined other campers walking down to the college campus with the hope of catching a glimpse of him. We melted into the throng of devoted followers gathered by the entrance to the gym. Most of the devotees were in their twenties and looked just like us, and we all eagerly awaited his presence. I was anxious to see the man who had appeared to me in Santa Barbara in his worldly form. We waited for an hour or more before an excited murmur swept through the crowd. Maharishi's car had been seen approaching. Finally, a white Plymouth convertible with the top down came into view. As it inched through the crowd of adoring fans, I recognized Jerry Jarvis, the man whom Maharishi had wanted to be my teacher. He was in the driver's seat, but I couldn't see Maharishi. Nonetheless, an elevated pitch of voices signaled that "the boss" had arrived. The car stopped and Jerry hurried around to open the passenger door.

Finally, Maharishi stepped out and I saw him.

Some experiences—often the best ones—are nearly impossible to put into words. The emotion I felt seeing Maharishi was one of those inexplicable moments. It was a recognition beyond time and thought, similar to the feeling I had during my first meditation. It was a relief to see him in the flesh. I felt as if I had finally come home to the place where I had always belonged. At a deeper level, there was no difference for me between the man who had spoken to me in the Volkswagen and the man I saw now. He was completely familiar to me so it hardly mattered what guise he took, but it was a validation, proof that he had not been only an apparition in Santa Barbara. Although Maharishi was only about five feet tall, his stature made him look taller. He had a regal bearing, standing with his back as straight if he had been in the military. I learned later that he was of the Kshatriya or warrior caste. No wonder I felt so taken. The way he walked—slowly and with such inherent dignity—took my breath away. He accepted flowers and said a few words to people he passed, leaving each one looking mesmerized. It was amazing to witness. Seeing others offering their flowers with so much love in their hearts, opened my own.

His presence confirmed for me that this man, clothed in a simple white garment, was holy. Maharishi embodied everything I longed for in a teacher. I had been imagining this moment, but it wasn't until I saw him in the flesh that I knew I was truly seeking him. There was nothing—no advanced warning—to let me know how profoundly I would be moved. Maharishi's presence validated my hope that there were beings on Earth who completely dedicated themselves to living a spiritual life. As he passed near to me, I felt a strong spiritual vibration, which I later learned is called "darshan."

This was a singular moment; one I had been waiting for. Fighting in a war had hardened me, something I wanted badly to rid myself of. I had experienced the worst of human anger and ferocity; now, I felt calmness and serenity. Since childhood I was convinced that there was more to life than what is seen on the surface. It was my deepest desire to know about the unseen, and now, here was a teacher who, in his gift of meditation, had already given me that experience. If there was anyone who might show me more, Maharishi was that person. He embodied the possibility of reconnecting with my deeper Self. Amazingly, just seeing Maharishi, gave me purpose and direction, and belief that the path I was beginning would lead me closer to him.

At the time I wasn't conscious of how powerful my connection to Maharishi was. The mystery of how he had found me in Santa Barbara, and seeing him now, was beyond my ability to comprehend. And yet, it created a longing, a yearning, for more, which meant I was no longer satisfied with life as it had been. I craved Maharishi's knowledge, although I had no idea how I knew—I just *knew*. I vowed to return as a registered participant if Maharishi returned to Humboldt next summer.

Birth of a Spiritual Seeker

My earliest memories are of trains. Although I was born in Manhattan, my parents lived in an apartment complex 30 miles outside the city in the suburb of Rye, New York. The place, called Country Gardens, was a magical wonderland in which to spend the first years of life. Two-story brick buildings faced lawns and flower gardens and a park across the street with a pond where my mother took me for walks in a carriage to feed the ducks. Children were everywhere in Country Gardens. The Hall and the Elgin families I remember best. Bitsy Elgin who was born on the same day as I was, became my first girlfriend. When we were three, we were caught naked in the bushes questioning the enigma of the human body. When my father found us, we learned we had breached the realm of acceptable human behavior.

My father was a strong presence in my life. He had

great success as creative director for an advertising agency in Manhattan, but his creativity extended beyond Madison Avenue. He transformed my simple bedroom into a cartoon wonderland by painting fantastical characters on the walls. But what was even more exciting to me were the lights from the passing trains on the New York, New Haven and Hartford Railroad. Country Gardens happened to be situated on a curve in the tracks so when a train came around the bend, the locomotive's light would shine through my bedroom window and light up my bedroom walls. Every time it happened it was the thrill of a lifetime.

My father explained what a train was and how the tracks outside connected with other tracks of other train lines that went to various places and connected the whole country. I am certain this helped catalyze my lifelong yearning for adventure. Where were these places that trains went? I wanted to visit them. Lights moving across my room set my imagination on fire, a fire that has never been extinguished. Would I grow up to be an engineer, or one of the brakemen that rode in the caboose at the end of the train? Or would the desire morph into something greater— something like self-discovery? I went to sleep each night listening to adventure stories my father made up in which I was a character. Tony climbs the Matterhorn or Tony sails around the world.

Once I finished high school, I flew to England with a school mate and we traveled through eight countries in Europe on motorcycles. Following that adventure, I've never stopped moving. My yearning to discover was not limited to seeing the physical world, it extended to discovering the unseen, the unknown. At some point I realized that the journey I was really on was a search for the meaning of life.

By the time I was a teenager, our family, which now included my younger sister, moved to Westport, Connecticut. It was due to my father's boundless imagination, that we were able to afford a nine-acre horse farm, complete with a steeplechase, stables, and a private tennis court. Our magnificent stone house, which he named Top o' the Hill, held expansive views of the countryside. At the time, Westport was at the far reaches of suburbia and attracted other creatives. Our neighbor on one side was the world-renowned sculptress Laura Garden Fraser, and on the other, the actor Paul Newman. It felt as if my home was merely an extension of my early fantasyland.

After school each day, I spent my time exploring nature, climbing trees, wandering the meadows and the woods on our property and beyond. I was blessed with plenty of alone-time to ponder. Taking after my art director father and painter mother, I was a visual thinker, which made it easy for me to imagine, not only what is seen in this world, but what is inside or beyond it. I didn't think it was unusual to lie on my back in the meadow and stare at a blade of grass, or sit for hours at the top of a maple tree. I was easily transported outside my mind to places where everything is beautiful, nothing hurts, nothing is mean or problematic, places of total perfection. I found that the deeper I sank into this perfect place, the happier I became. I knew that I wanted to be there. I wanted to be there permanently.

There was really no one except my sister who could understand, so I didn't talk about this with anyone else. When playing with my close friends, we'd just do what kids do. We swam and built rafts in the river at the bottom of our hill. We made carts to sail down the hill in the summer and skied down it in the winter. But when I was by myself, which I didn't mind at all, I could appreciate more of the blessed silence around me. Being by myself, I knew there was more to the world than just what appeared on the surface. Being alone was when I began to discover things. I learned that when I really looked at something—really looked into it—more would be revealed. And the more I looked, the more that was revealed.

Years later, I learned from Maharishi that "seeking more and more" is the natural direction of life. Everyone desires greater *something*, especially greater happiness. Maharishi's Transcendental Meditation is based on this simple law of nature: When the mind is left alone, it will seek a place of greater happiness. It automatically goes toward more and more.

For me, seeing deeper into things raised questions the mind couldn't answer. I began to realize there was much more that couldn't be answered than could. My questions inspired even deeper questions until one day I thought I had reached the most basic question of all: What is? In other words, what exists?

For years, I pursued an answer to this question. I discovered the spiritual section in Klein's bookstore on Main Street in Westport, actual books for spiritual seekers, people who didn't believe life was just the way it appeared on the surface, and wanted to look deeper. The first book I bought was *The Way of Zen*, by D. T. Suzuki. I immediately was struck by the Ten Oxherder Drawings, which describe the Zen training path to enlightenment, folk images with poems and commentaries. In fact, I found myself in them. It was the story of me—*my* life.

Alone in the wilderness, lost in the jungle, the boy is searching, searching. The swelling waters, the far-away mountains, and the unending path; exhausted and in despair, he knows not where to go, he only hears the evening cicadas singing in the maple-woods.

The ten drawings, taken together, elucidate a person's life. More importantly, they confirmed for me that there is a reason why we had arrived on this planet in a human body.

He now knows that vessels, however varied, are all of gold, and that the objective world is a reflection of the self.

I had suspected all along that the world was my creation, that I made it happen every moment. But now, it was being confirmed by an ancient Zen master, Kaku-an Shien.

The drawings show the arc from birth to death, or from being Pure Consciousness, to experiencing the illusion of existence, to returning to Pure Consciousness. I loved it. It made life simple, simple as a blade of grass moving in the wind.

The *Way of Zen* inspired me to return often to the narrow aisle in the back of Klein's. Over time, I found more books that confirmed things for me and helped me to navigate the spiritual world. There were mostly books on Zen and the life of Buddha that I especially loved reading about. There were even some books listed under Catholicism that got my attention. I related to the experiences of Saint Teresa of Avila, a great mystic who wrote about spirituality in the 16th century, and Saint John the Divine, apostle of Jesus. I was excited to find that there were deep thinkers even within my family's religion, the Roman Catholic

Church. *The Cloud of Unknowing,* a Middle Ages anonymous work of Christian mysticism, opened up a door for me. It let me know that everything can't be explained with logic. That the mind wasn't able to understand the deepest meaning of things. The more I thought, the more it seemed that the mind was quite an imperfect thing. In fact, its ultimate reasoning could be utterly ridiculous.

It was the 1960's, a time of huge transition. Our country had entered a war on the other side of the world. More and more, life was proving its utter insanity. I was attracted to Albert Camus and Jean Paul Sartre for a time, purveyors of the uselessness of life, although I personally held a much more positive view. I had seen the deep beauty contained beneath the surface and realized that was the direction to follow. After all, Jesus told us that the kingdom of heaven existed within us.

The year I graduated from prep school, I finally found the *Upanishads,* sacred Hindu texts, my first Indian classic, and it was filled with answers to my deepest questions. There seemed to be an answer on every page. The *Kena Upanishad* begins by asking my questions—

Who sends the mind to wander afar? Who first drives life to start on its journey? Who impels us to utter these words? Who is the Spirit behind the eye and the ear?

And answering them—

It is the ear of the ear, the eyes of the eyes, and the Word of words, the mind of mind, and the life of life. Those who follow wisdom pass beyond and, on leaving this world, become immortal.

From the *Upanishads: There the eye goes not, nor words, nor mind.*

We know not, we cannot understand, how he can be explained: He is above the known and he is above the unknown. This have we heard from the ancient sages who explained this truth to us.

What cannot be spoken with words, but that whereby words are spoken: Know that alone to be Brahman, the Spirit; and not what people here adore.

I often had tears in my eyes in the back aisle in Klein's, because I had found the words for what I always knew to be true. It was beyond beautiful to find there were others from time immemorial who knew these truths. Knowing I was not alone was comforting and freeing and gave me courage to believe in a spiritual path.

War Trauma

My sudden intense zealousness to be with Maharishi created a rift in my relationship with Gloria, who didn't feel the same pull, and we struggled with our differing paths. Gloria was completely self-sufficient and was not looking for a teacher. She was satisfied reading Henry Miller and Anais Nin, playing her guitar and singing Joni Mitchell songs. She was a simple, natural person who felt no need to be seeking and questioning. By contrast, my thirst for spiritual knowledge, fueled by questions created by the war, was overwhelming. After seeing Maharishi, returning to our normal life proved difficult. Thoreau, our sweet puppy, was the catalyst that changed our direction. While staying as guests on a commune in Oregon, Thoreau wandered into a field where he was kicked by a horse and seriously injured. To pay the vet bill, we were forced to sell the van and decided to move to the East Coast for a fresh start.

We bought train tickets from Oregon to Seattle, to Vancouver, where we booked seats for the transcontinental train to Montreal, and from there we hitched a ride south. Landing in Vermont, we lucked into a job caretaking a log cabin in Vermont on 300 acres of land with an enchanted birch forest and a view of the Green Mountains. Gloria cooked and bound small books which she filled with watercolor sketches and Thoreau ran through the birches with animal delight.

But what I couldn't anticipate was that the quiet surroundings brought on nightmares of the war. I thought meditation would help rid me of them, so when I wasn't working at a neighbor's business dismantling barns, I meditated non-stop, unaware of the consequences. I began to release stress at an alarming rate, and although I was mostly calm, the simplest disagreements would trigger bouts of anger. With non-stop nightmares that fractured my sleep, I had no idea what was happening to me. Closing my eyes at night meant diving into a sea of ominous moving shapes that would transform into monsters so terrifying and overwhelming that I'd have to open my eyes to escape. I had night sweats and day sweats. I suffered from hypertension and hypervigilance but, worst of all were the bouts of uncontrollable rage, which made life very difficult for Gloria. I was a combat veteran suffering from the symptoms of Post-Traumatic Stress Disorder and didn't know it. I remembered what Hans Sebbelov told me on the pier in Santa Barbara: "The worst wounds are those that effect the mind." But that didn't make the horror go away. He had set me on the path toward Maharishi, but now I was as far away from him as I had ever been.

Gloria and I moved in with my parents in Connecticut where I checked myself into the Veterans Administration Hospital in New Haven. The place was overwhelmed by soldiers returning from Vietnam, many with physical injuries, easier to diagnose than mental wounds. The doctors had no idea what to do with cases like mine. Because of the over-crowding, they put me in the amputee ward where we awakened early every morning by someone strapped to a gurney screaming as he was wheeled out to surgery. I was screaming inwardly; no one could hear me. To prevent trauma victims from acting out, they tranquilized us with pain killers. I became so drugged up that one day on the way to the shower, I walked face-first into a wall. The doctors, who were looking for physical, not psychological reasons, as a cause for my symptoms, finally blamed my behavior on a hyper thyroid. Their answer was to cut out three-quarters of the organ, a procedure I refused. They released me from the hospital with medication to slow my thyroid function while offering little expectation of a cure.

Searching for a solution, we moved back to California in the hope of returning to the normal life we had there. We rented an apartment above a garage in Santa Barbara. I found a job, again in a bookstore, this one among the exclusive El Paseo shops, and Gloria worked as a waitress in a restaurant. But moving didn't help and our relationship continued to suffer. Things became even more untenable when we invited Gloria's brother to move in with us. Davey had just returned from Vietnam addicted to heroin, and foolishly, we thought we could help him kick his habit. Instead, he stole from us and never got clean. My frustration with him triggered my own war trauma, which continued to flare up in bouts of anger. Once again, I turned to long meditations to calm myself. I hid from the constant tumult by meditating in a walk-in closet. Interactions between the three of us became so volatile that I insanely thought I could heal Davey by praying for him while deep in meditation. I called upon my childhood god, Jesus Christ, to aid me, and vowed that I would not stop meditating until he appeared to me. Sinking deep into meditation while praying to see Jesus, I begged with such fervor that suddenly I had a clear vision of myself as a baby in my mother's arms beside the sea of Galilee. Jesus, wearing a brown robe, came down a hill towards us. With his acolytes behind him, he stopped in front of us and lifted me from my mother's arms and held me. There were no words spoken, but the vision was overwhelmingly powerful.

Unfortunately, my "vision" morphed into a crazy "born again" experience but was not at all successful in healing Davey. The idea popped into my head that I should dress in white and sink into meditation whenever and wherever I could. One day after meditating beneath a tree in the park, a homeless man picking through a trash bin for food inspired me to feed the homeless. I bought loaves of bread, made peanut butter and jelly sandwiches, and took them to where the homeless camped by the railroad tracks.

My fervor was short-lived but the situation in our small apartment remained unsustainable. Finally, we evicted Davey, but that didn't change the relationship between Gloria and me. She had begun staying out late at night singing at a club in town with an Irish folk band. Waking one morning, I found a note for me by the bed. She was moving to Ireland with the band. Devastated,

I sank to a place even lower than when Maharishi had first come to me. I was deeply distraught and could hardly eat. I started smoking cigarettes and drinking non-stop. To save myself, I flew East and moved back in with my parents. In the comfort and safety of their home, my life began to stabilize. I returned to meditating for the recommended time, twenty minutes morning and evening. My life began to regain balance. I quit smoking, cut my shoulder length hair, shaved my beard. I found a simple job. And, finally, in deference to Maharishi's instructions a year ago, I gave up women.

Then the unexpected happened and everything changed.

Maharishi and the Generals

*D*avid Rottenberg called me from Boston. Surprise turned into amazement at how much he had changed. Our lives had gone full circle in a single year. We had driven to California together and learned to meditate together. We lost touch when I left with Gloria, and now we were both back on the East Coast. He had taken a teacher training course with Maharishi in Italy and was teaching at the Cambridge Transcendental Meditation Center. He had become one of the people I'd admired at the Westwood Center, and spoke with the bliss of a TM Teacher. When he told me that Maharishi was coming to give a talk at the Massachusetts Institute of Technology, I couldn't believe the luck of my timing. The opportunity had come out of nowhere, bringing me back to Maharishi when I least expected it.

We arrived early for Maharishi's talk and found seats in the second row of the auditorium. In the center of the stage was a gold upholstered couch in front of the same picture of Guru Dev, Maharishi's teacher, that was on the altar for my initiation. There was a table with two chairs behind it on the right side of the stage. The expectation of Maharishi's appearance energized the hall. I leaned forward, anticipating hearing the sound of his voice.

Suddenly, there was a collective gasp from the audience when two U.S. Army generals in full dress uniform walked onstage and took seats at the table accompanied by hissing and booing from the audience. For the ultra-liberal Cambridge student population, the generals represented everything considered evil about the United States government. Anti-war protesters across the country were railing against Army generals as warmongers, part of the military-industrial complex.

But the generals were something very different for the soldier in me. I was in awe. The gold stars on their shoulders sparkling under the stage lights filled me with pride. The situation, so unexpected, was complicated for me. My mind, cracked open by Vietnam, was still fragile. Only a year ago, I had returned from a war that I didn't sign up for, but was drafted by my country to fight. I had done my duty and had medals to prove it. But Vietnam was a war nobody wanted, certainly not those of us who had been there. Still, I had the utmost respect for my fellow warriors, some of whom never came back. I had a deep emotional attachment for the role soldiers play.

The rank of general represented the highest value of being a warrior, something I knew wasn't felt by most of the audience. Instead, the emotion in the hall felt more like an impending storm. I heard the people seated around me questioning why an Indian yogi, supposedly a man of peace, would invite these "warmongers" to share his stage. While we all waited for Maharishi, the generals sat silent. I was aware that David, knowing how I felt, was uncomfortable as well, trapped as he was, between me and a rancorous crowd.

After leaving enough time for his visual message to sink in, Maharishi walked proudly onstage smiling blissfully, dressed in a white silk dhoti holding an armful of flowers. The embodiment of self-confidence, he moved in the regal way that had captured me at Humboldt. The look on his joy-filled face spoke volumes: all was right in heaven and on earth—in fact, everything was perfect. The murmuring stopped while his assistant, a young bearded Indian, also dressed in a dhoti, placed a deerskin on the couch. Meanwhile, Maharishi paused in front of the generals to say a few words, handing each of them a white carnation. The booing started up again. It was 1970 and the war was still raging in Vietnam. This was Cambridge, Massachusetts, home of Harvard and Boston University and MIT and other nearby colleges and universities, the center of the antiwar movement for the East Coast. The unspoken question still on everyone's mind was, what was Maharishi doing sharing a stage with two army generals? As he took his seat on the couch, I felt anxious and protective of him. I assumed the booing members of the audience had no idea how great the sacrifice soldiers make by risking their lives. I felt alone in the center of the auditorium.

While Maharishi settled himself on the couch, a young man with long hair approached the audience microphone. He identified himself as a reporter for the *Boston Free Press*, the alternative newspaper that condemned the war, and asked the question that was on everyone's mind.

"Maharishi, how can you call yourself a man of peace while you share the stage with these warmongers?"

A loud cheer resounded throughout the hall as if the young man was the voice for the entire audience. I remained silent, feeling I had no voice, and shrank quietly within myself. I could feel the charged energy in the air on my skin. When Maharishi spoke, his voice barely audible over the speakers, his words sunk deep into me.

He said, "Being a soldier is the highest calling a man can have. Because it asks him to sacrifice his life for a higher cause."

His answer, both unapologetic and truthful, shocked everyone and it earned him my undying respect. Maharishi made no excuses. He took the journalist's question, used it as ammunition, and exploded it in plain sight. I am positive that the reporter was expecting some lame excuse, when instead, he got a dose of truth. Not only did Maharishi recognize the deepest reality of being a warrior, he honored the generals and, at least, one other man in the room. For the first time since returning home, I felt that my decision to go to war had been validated. I had always believed I had done the right thing by showing up and going to Vietnam. Now here, filled with emotion, I heard Maharishi affirming it.

The booing subsided and even a few cheers burst out in the audience. Maharishi, having spoken the truth, cut through the controversy of whether or not the war in Vietnam was justified. His statement took no side—instead, he spoke to a deeper reality. Having witnessed Maharishi's integrity, I was now certain I would follow him anywhere. Leaving the hall, the light was brighter outside, just as it was on Gayley Avenue after my first meditation.

Maharishi would be teaching at Humboldt again that summer. So, I was blessed with a second chance.

Humboldt

his time I had a plan when I arrived for the six-week
advanced meditation course: I would be a paying participant.
I soon realized how much I had changed over the past year—I
perceived things more clearly. Somehow, a year ago, I had missed
the exceptional beauty of the Humboldt College campus with
its rows of flowers lining the streets and paths. I now felt I had
arrived at the place I was meant to be—with Maharishi. Thinking
of this made me feel privileged and elated, yet, I feared I wouldn't
fit in. I was hyper-aware of the people around me and felt shy
about being among those that appeared to be such seasoned
spiritual seekers.

I noticed two groups that I would recognize at future
courses as fixtures: One was the permanent staff who ran the
nuts and bolts of the event and were shown deference because

of their closeness to the master, something I could never imagine for myself. I was intimidated by the way they spoke with a sense of owning some precious knowledge inaccessible to the rest of us. In contrast, were the zealots who sold pictures of Maharishi taken at courses in India and rare photos of Guru Dev. They also sold trinkets and incense and they claimed front seats and waited for Maharishi for hours, with flowers in hand. If he smiled at them or said a few words they were blissed out and could be overheard talking about the encounter for days. Watching their theatrical display of devotion struck me the wrong way, and I promised myself I would never become one of them.

I came to the course with a genuine seed of love for Maharishi planted deep in my heart. It was something I couldn't explain, but was very real. I had heard that merely being in the presence of an enlightened master—in his "darshan"—has a powerful effect, but still I didn't feel ready to be close to him. Being in that refined atmosphere alone, was enough to make me uncomfortable. My intense shyness made me want to be invisible, and out of fear of being noticed, I chose to sit in the back of the hall as far away from Maharishi as possible.

My discomfort was caused by a release of stress, something I'd become familiar with when I meditated for too long. And that stress included the guilt I felt because of persistent images of war that overwhelmed me. Even in this space dedicated to creating a deeply spiritual life, the war continued to rage on in my head. When Maharishi entered the hall and the atmosphere began to settle down, flashbacks would begin. They made me feel isolated from the others—the blissed-out, soft-spoken meditators around me. If they only knew what was going on inside me, I was sure I would be ushered out of the hall and banished from the course. There were times when I questioned whether I belonged on the course at all. Seated far in the back of the audience, I pictured myself with an M-16 in my hands mowing down the audience from behind. I was ashamed. I wanted to be anyone but that maniac, but stopping it was beyond my control. It would happen and then be over and I would pray that it wouldn't happen again.

But it would.

Even from a distance, I was certain Maharishi knew what was going on inside me. I felt so terrible that I didn't want him to see me. Several times, I stood up and crept out of the hall. Thankfully, the episodes grew rarer as the course progressed and eventually I was able to submerge myself with the others into the sublime atmosphere created by Maharishi's presence. Maharishi spoke in simple terms that even a shattered soldier with a limited attention span could understand. To meditate, he said, was to "Water the root to enjoy the fruit," and "Capture the fort to win all the surrounding territory." He was telling us that by practicing Transcendental Meditation, we nurture the core of our life. And nurturing the core affects every aspect of our life—the surrounding territory—for the better.

I kept to the course routine as best as I could. When we were not in the lectures, most of our time was spent "rounding." One round consisted of a simple breathing exercise called pranayama, a twenty-minute meditation followed by fifteen minutes of simple yoga postures—asanas—to stretch the muscles. The rounds were done one after the other from morning until noon with a break for lunch and then resumed until dinner and Maharishi's evening talk. When it became too onerous, I gave myself permission to lace up my hiking boots and trek through the redwood forest behind the college where I felt most comfortable, in nature. I also explored the town of Arcata. I loved the way the traditional California cottages lined the streets and the quaint central square.

Arcata's harbor had a fleet of salmon boats and a selection of funky bars and cafés. I chanced upon a café frequented by other course participants who had also escaped rounding. There I met a woman, intelligent and striking, who was both an artist and a longtime meditator. Francesca, who had been with Maharishi in India, was exceptionally grounded in his knowledge, and she enjoyed explaining the parts of his teachings I found difficult to understand. Confessing to experiencing overload and skipping out of meetings herself, she made me feel that I wasn't alone.

Meeting the other participants became nearly as important as sitting in the lecture hall. As my shyness began to dissolve, my interactions with some longtime meditators helped me realize that I was, indeed, a novice in my spiritual quest. But this wasn't necessarily a bad thing. Being a novice meant there were possibilities of priceless unfoldment ahead, and endless riches to be revealed. I could expect unending realizations about life by staying on the path.

Luckily, without trying, I was able to hold Maharishi in my heart. I trusted in the master-disciple relationship without the need to plumb the depths and understand all the intricacies of his teaching. As time passed, I became more and more convinced that it wasn't the knowledge that was important, it was one's relationship with the master himself. In the end, my naiveté is what led me and allowed me to progress on the spiritual path. I came to understand that I couldn't be anyone different from who I was. We all had our separates paths, and it was a relief to realize I couldn't be anyone other than myself. As Maharishi once said, "Know what you are, and know that you are what you've been looking for."

I had already experienced healthy chunks of life. I had a strong sense of right and wrong and well-developed survival skills. I had grown up spending my summers sailing a large wooden yawl on the Atlantic, and once sailed through a hurricane. After prep school, I rode a motorcycle through Europe and maneuvered through unexpected situations. And then, there was my year in the infantry in Vietnam. I had learned that the intellect wasn't everything. Deep in my heart, I knew that life itself was the greatest teacher. But experience had taught me that life wasn't what *I thought* it would be. Nothing ever turned out as I *expected*. Life seemed mysterious and constantly changing which made me want to look deeper, to go underneath for something real and solid to hang on to.

I began to recognize that Maharishi, with his expanded consciousness, was the only one who could guide me flawlessly through life. Besides, he had found me—and that had happened for a reason. I felt it must be my good fortune—my good karma—that delivered me here. Yet, my thinking mind sowed uncertainty. I realized that my mind was as changeable as the weather, which is why I had such strong faith in the process of going within. Inside, where the non-changing state of Pure Being resides is where "nature would organize" as I heard Maharishi say one day. But still, on the surface, my mind created an endless string of doubts about everything. This included whether or not I belonged on an advanced meditation course.

Or even, whether or not I should be a follower of Maharishi's at all.

Maharishi Talks About Armor

As my head cleared, thanks to the course, I continued to hear more of what Maharishi was telling us. I found there were actually times when Maharishi's words rang within me clear as a bell. In one lecture, he defined in simple terms how Transcendental Meditation works. He used archery as an analogy, equating the process of transcending to pulling back the bow string and, the moment of returning to normal awareness, to letting the arrow fly. The pulling back is analogous to the restful state of meditation, while the arrow flying is moving into activity. In other words, the state of Pure Being we access in meditation "flies" out and lands in our waking life. He told us that only five percent of the Being we experience in meditation remains in activity—until, that is, we attain Cosmic Consciousness. In my recent experience, I wasn't sure that I retained even five percent.

If I was being perfectly honest, I sometimes wasn't at all sure that I even transcended. It was Maharishi's encouragement that kept me meditating regularly. Whenever I heard him speak, I never doubted that I would keep meditating and eventually, I would bring enough of the silence in meditation into activity. He gently assured us that when cosmic intelligence remains constant during activity, every action will become bliss.

When Maharishi stood up and walked off the stage that day, I floated out of the hall and headed for the redwood grove behind the college, the same grove Gloria and I had camped in the year before. But now, I was floating on a blissful wave with the sound of Maharishi's voice still in my head. Now, whenever I listened to Maharishi speak, I seemed to surf on a wave of his bliss. I knew Maharishi was the source of that bliss and that it would draw me back to him again and again.

As I walked along the soft mossy floor beneath the trees with Maharishi still with me, I heard him saying that in Cosmic Consciousness, the mind takes on a kind of armor that protects us from taking on any stress and strain. For all time, the armor will protect us so that no bullets can get through. A smile broke out on my face. I felt that Maharishi had been talking to me alone as a soldier. But then I thought, that maybe I am no longer a soldier, but have graduated to being a "spiritual warrior."

The Analogy of Watching a Movie

A few weeks into the course, I was comfortable enough to move closer to the front of the auditorium, to a place where I could see Maharishi almost life-size. There was a microphone on a stand set up at the base of the stage where course participants could come forward and ask questions. I was still far too shy to ask a question myself, but someone would often ask my question for me. As I learned later, this was a common phenomenon, not mine alone. One of the first times this happened, a young woman stepped up to the microphone and told Maharishi that she experienced transcending with her eyes open.

Maharishi smiled and said, "It is like nearing the goal. You are still on the path yet seeing the goal."

Later, a young man asked this: "Maharishi, I heard you say that on the path to realization, a man must experience himself as separate from the world, as witness to it."

Maharishi answered, "It will be good to establish the ground first. Then, on this ground, we raise the trees and buildings. Thus, on the path of enlightenment, it is necessary to experience the separateness. What is the state of enlightenment? What is the path to enlightenment? Enlightenment can be defined as lack of ignorance. In itself, it should be fullness of knowledge. Fullness of experience. If one is enlightened it means he knows everything there is to know. He has experienced everything there is to be experienced. Life is abundant, infinite, boundary-less. Unbounded. The path to this state is from individual awareness to unbounded."

He glanced down at the flower in his hand. "When the awareness of the viewer is contained within the *boundary* of the flower," he said, pointing to the petals, "this is *individual* perception. When perception is individual, the awareness is overtaken by the object, in this case, the flower. When the see-er cannot maintain himself as a witness, his awareness is overtaken, and Pure Awareness is not available. The white color of a cinema screen is another example. White is the true color of the screen, but a picture, with its colors, covers it. In this way, the picture dominates, and the real nature of the screen is not available. At the cost of the nature of the screen, the cinema is enjoyed. The perceptions of the world, the infinite perceptions, are all enjoyed at the cost of the real nature of the enjoyer. The enjoyer himself is—we use the word, bound."

After about three hours when the session ended, I left the hall feeling once again like I was floating in an ocean of bliss. This wasn't my common experience and yet, somehow it felt familiar. Although it was time to head back to our rooms for meditation I couldn't go. I was steered past my dormitory and up a hill to the familiar path through the redwood grove behind the campus. I felt energized enough to explode and needed the calming effect of nature.

As I floated beneath the majestic trees, with my head filled with Maharishi's words, I replayed the part of the meeting I remembered, when he explained that, in the state of ignorance, we are in bondage. He used the word "bound," which stuck in my mind and caused me to envision my normal state of mind. I saw that I was, most definitely, *bound.* I knew that I had been living my life being bound by everything I encountered.

Maharishi had made it so clear. We live our lives ignorant of our own infinite value. We lose our infinite value by enjoying the limited value. Nothing could be truer. I knew that I lived my life not knowing the infinite cosmic being I really am. Once again, he used the example of watching a movie in which the whiteness of the screen on which the film is being shown, is continually being overshadowed by the images we are watching.

While this was in my mind, I was given a real-life example that I was living in the moment. I saw that I had been overtaken by the majesty of the trees around me, and had lost any sense of self.

A squirrel scurried up to me until he saw that he had mistaken my leg for a tree trunk. I laughed and realized I had been standing perfectly still for an unknown amount of time. I had not been looking out through my eyes, but instead looking inward. My eyes were open and I was seeing a kind of hazy view of the forest and yet, somehow, my infinite nature had not been lost. It may have only been for a few seconds but the moment was timeless. My perception had not overshadowed me. My true nature, the whiteness of the screen, was not lost.

With a smile on my face, I headed back to my room. I understood then that Maharishi was not talking in the abstract; his message was very real.

When the course was over, I became eligible for a training course with Maharishi in Spain to become a TM teacher. Although I had no desire to teach, attending the course was my way to remain close to Maharishi. I returned to Connecticut, found a job on the loading dock of a computer company, and made enough money to cover my expenses.

Armed with the course fee and an airline ticket to Spain, I was on my way.

La Antilla

I was *A Stranger in a Strange Land*, like the boy in Robert Heinlein's book of that name, who came to Earth after having been born on Mars. This was myself showing up for Maharishi's teacher training course in Spain. Two-thousand spiritual seekers from Europe and America landed in La Antilla, a small seaside town of white-washed haciendas built in the Moorish style along a beach on the Atlantic Coast south of Seville.

I arrived knowing next to nothing about what was to come. There was no advanced curriculum and all we knew was that Maharishi was going to train us to become teachers of Transcendental Meditation. I hadn't been in school for years and was nervous about what the learning might involve. My most recent education had been in Advanced Infantry Training at Fort Jackson, South Carolina where I had earned the job description of

11B40—Light Weapons Infantry Specialist. The contrast couldn't be greater. I didn't know it at the time, but having no direction, in an expanded cosmic sense, was the perfect qualification for being a willing candidate for Maharishi's teachings. Humboldt had given me a gentle nudge along a spiritual path that was slowly becoming visible to me. Now, I was more convinced than ever that my direction led to Maharishi. Teacher Training proved to be my first deep dive into his knowledge. At Humboldt I'd been so filled with angst that I retained very little. Nothing in my experience so far had prepared me for the depth and beauty of what was about to unfold.

Most of the 2,000 participants were about my age, in their early twenties, although there was also a small, but wise-looking, contingent of white-haired elders. As much as I wanted to fit in, I still felt like an outsider. And I looked like one in the standard preppy-from-Connecticut uniform of khakis and button-down shirts. Almost everyone else dressed like a spiritual seeker in embroidered cotton shirts and loose yoga pants. Some men wore Indian kurtas and women wore long cotton skirts. These outfits led me to believe that they had been to India and were farther along than I was on the spiritual path. My year in an infantry battalion in a South Vietnamese jungle was about as far away from India, spiritually speaking, as one could get. It took me a long time to let go of the idea that I was a novice compared to everyone else. But I was as wrong about that as I was about other stereotypes. After meeting enough people, I realized that it made no sense to compare myself with others. It was nonsensical to judge anyone's spirituality by the clothes they wore.

I shared a single-story Moorish-style bungalow, with whitewashed walls and red tile floors, with two other participants. We spent most of every day in our rooms meditating or doing yoga asanas while staring at the walls, the floor and the ceiling. It was the same routine we followed at Humboldt: one meditation followed by a set of asanas and a few minutes of pranayama breathing exercise, repeated for most of the day. We attended classes to learn teaching techniques, and were given the task of writing our own introductory and preparatory lectures. When the schedule became too onerous, the beach was just a block away. Although, for the most part, I found my meditations quite blissful, I still spent a fair amount of time walking along the ocean.

The most special part of our day was the time spent with Maharishi each evening in the packed lobby of a hotel. I made a point of always being among the first to arrive so I could secure a seat up front and on the floor. I wanted to be as close to Maharishi as possible. The time I spent sitting on the hard terrazzo floor, squeezed between pairs of shoulders like an anchovy in a can, listening to Maharishi speak was precious. I was a sponge soaking up his priceless knowledge. No matter what the subject, I reveled in his words. The moment he entered, always walking in his dignified way, with an infinite smile on his face, I knew there was no place on the planet I would rather be. Being in the master's presence turned the hot and stuffy hotel lobby into a holy sanctuary. When Maharishi's gaze happened to land on me, I would feel a giddy rush of bliss that would last for hours. I couldn't deny it; I'd become the fanatic I swore I would never be.

I took detailed notes intent on understanding Maharishi's

every word. Slowly, I was finding answers to my deepest and most burning questions. Although I was still too afraid to step up to a microphone to ask a question, I was always amazed to hear someone else ask it for me. By now I knew this was a universal experience: People in the presence of an enlightened master become of one collective mind. More and more the audience burst into laughter when a situation was mentioned that was obviously universal. It was as if there existed only one mind.

We often sat late into the night while I scribbled Maharishi's every word into my notebook. I had gone through a huge transformation since Humboldt. No longer was I hiding in the back row, I became comfortable sitting at the feet of the master, and realized that just being in that crowded room sitting at the master's feet was a privilege earned over lifetimes. I was acutely aware of the preciousness of every breath I took in Maharishi's presence. The intensity and unboundedness of the experience cannot be exaggerated. Maharishi's words were not heard channeled through my intellect; his knowledge was instilled in a deeper way. Years afterward—even now—his words remain vibrant and alive in my consciousness and surface whenever needed.

My blue course notebook had Maharishi's picture printed on the cover along with the words, "The Science of Creative Intelligence," which is how Maharishi characterized the knowledge at the time. Always refining his message to meet the needs of specific periods of time, in subsequent years he would change the titles, but his message always remained the same.

Taken from my notes, the basic principles of Maharishi's teachings are:

The nature of life is to progress, evolve and grow towards fulfillment.

The cause of suffering is weakness and weakness is eliminated through the development of creative intelligence.

Creative intelligence is located at the source of thought.

To sustain progress, we must be more creative, day by day.

To be more creative every day, we must draw upon the reservoir of creative intelligence by meditating twice a day.

Thus, rest (meditation), and activity are the steps of progress.

The two aspects of the science of creative intelligence are knowledge and experience.

This last point resonated deeply because I knew from my own life experience that theoretical knowledge alone was never enough. Knowledge had to be combined with experience to be complete. In the army I'd learned that all the myriad battle-preparedness classes in training turned out to be so much fluff the moment I was shot at for the first time.

Maharishi often answered questions from the audience. At times, the conversations could become very subtle and abstract. The realization that I was taking in his words on a more subtle level gave me the confidence to go even deeper. Deeper levels of understanding began to unfold in my daily life. I began to notice that at times my thoughts would materialize. I would think something and it would happen. This took place only in Maharishi's presence at first, but later at random times. For example, I would think of someone and instantly they would appear.

Although the topics of Maharishi's lectures were unlimited, the subtext was always self-awareness. He spoke beautifully of the quiet realm we experience in meditation. *"Self-awareness describes something we don't have to possess anew. It is the area that is always quiet so we call it unbounded awareness. Self-aware because it is the area within, not something we have to get."*

I realized that I had been experiencing this silence since childhood, that it was nothing new. But his description was so clear that it allowed me to *own* the knowledge. It became part of me.

And it was beyond beautiful.

Often, when Maharishi mentioned something it would invoke a remembrance from the past, as if what he was pointing to was some knowledge that was asleep and just needed to be awakened. "A time comes when we become a close intimate friend of *yogastha karu karmani* (steadfast practice)" he said. "From the Bhagavad Gita, it is said, 'Be steadfast in yoga, oh, Arjuna. Perform your duty and abandon all attachment to success or failure. Such evenness of mind is called yoga.'" When he said, "Then it never leaves us; we are one with it always," I knew I was listening to him describe the knowledge I had been seeking all my life. Moreover, I realized he was speaking of his own state of consciousness.

Maharishi had a way of making the most abstract subject easy to grasp. "It's like having glasses on our eyes; we're looking through them, and then someone tells us we have them on. Then we can say, 'Oh, I am That' when we see the unbounded. But not only That which is the Unmanifest (the field of Pure Consciousness) but 'I am This'—the Manifest (the material world). Then, all This is That!" We can encompass both.

Again, I felt as if Maharishi was giving me what, for lifetimes, I had ached for. The whole process beginning in Santa Barbara had a feeling of inevitability and a sense that there was no going back. There was no returning to a softer, gentler way of evolving; I was strapped into my seat in the rocket ship and there was no escaping as we hurtled through space. Being in Teacher Training and being constantly in Maharishi's darshan, life was exaggerated. Ups and downs were greater. I would be intensely happy one day and just the opposite the next. Sometimes things were progressing so rapidly, it seemed that no matter how fast I ran, I couldn't keep up.

The work became more challenging as the course progressed. There was a lot of memorization of various aspects of teaching including the puja and the remainder of the initiation ceremony when mantras are imparted. The most difficult part was memorizing incredibly detailed instructions called The Checking Notes. To assure meditations remained effortless for students, we had to recall dozens of pages that would cover any possible questions a new initiate might have. At times, I became so overwhelmed I feared I wouldn't be able to complete the work. This insecurity pulled me in different directions. First, there was the undeniable feeling that I belonged with Maharishi and that there was probably no one else on Earth who could give me what I wanted. I never doubted my respect and unbridled love for him and yet, there were still times when I doubted that I belonged there at all. I couldn't escape who I was, or who I thought I was, because of whom I had been—among other things, a soldier in Vietnam. For the most part, Vietnam had faded but it had an insidious way of surfacing whenever it pleased. The more positive I felt, the more negativity rushed in to balance it. The words "baby killer" could still ring in my head.

My lowest point during the course occurred with an assignment to write an introductory lecture for students and then read it in front of about 200 course members. The first steps in teaching Transcendental Meditation begin with these introductory lectures. Each of us was asked to stand at a podium, speak over a microphone, and give the first five minutes of the lecture we had written. When it was my turn, I stood on the stage, heard my voice say "hello" over the speakers, and froze with fright. I couldn't speak another word. I picked up my notes and walked off, humiliated. A few days later, a kind course leader gently offered me a second chance. I politely refused, telling him I knew I wouldn't be able to do it. It was a given.

I thought for sure I had flunked Teacher Training.

Becoming a TM Teacher

At the start of the morning meeting on the second-to-last day of the course, Jerry Jarvis stepped onstage with a list of those Maharishi had selected to become teachers. This implied that some wouldn't be on it and I thought for sure that I would be one of them. Why wouldn't I? After all, I couldn't speak a single word of my Introductory Lecture. When I heard Jerry read my name, I assumed there must be some mistake. Had no one noticed that I couldn't give my lecture? Without the lecture, how could I teach TM? Why had my pitiful performance been overlooked? I wondered if Maharishi had given me a pass, or maybe no one had bothered to tell him about the debacle. I tried to see the positive side. After all, I had memorized the checking notes and the puja, but that was not the entire goal. The list of soon-to-be-teachers was posted in the basement hallway of the hotel near the classrooms. I rushed down there when the meeting was over to confirm that my name was really on the list or if Jerry had made some mistake. But there it was, along with the hour I was to meet with Maharishi to be made a teacher. Nine o'clock the next morning—I still couldn't believe it was happening.

I arrived in the dark hallway in the basement just before 9:00 a.m. A woman on staff was seated at a table outside one of the classrooms. I gave her my name and watched intensely while she ran the point of a ballpoint pen down the list on the desk. I thought there still might be a chance that an error had been made, and she would look up dolefully and say, "I'm sorry, we can't find your name on the list." But that didn't happen. After I watched her put a checkmark beside my name, she looked up at me and smiled. Only then did I finally believe.

At that moment, I felt a very subtle, very deep realization that everything was taking place in some new way I wasn't prepared for, as if my experience was happening on "another level altogether, without my help." I did know that things were unfolding because of a power greater than myself and that I was powerless over that and over the outcome. I was merely the witness watching myself acting in this play. Although I hadn't flunked the course, I hadn't *not* flunked, either. Something else, something other than my will to make things happen, had decided to give me a pass. Wasn't this what Maharishi had been telling us all along? That we are constantly taking credit for what Mother Nature is doing. The way I understood it, in Cosmic Consciousness one's perspective changes, so we witness what we are doing from an unbounded, cosmic, point of view.

So, only then would we understand we are not the doers. I had caused myself a lot of anxiety by creating unnecessary drama when the reality was, I had nothing to do with the outcome. I'd done all that worrying for nothing.

I took a deep breath.

Behind the young woman was a pair of glass double-doors covered with sheets. One of Maharishi's secretaries, an energetic young man in a dark blue suit, rushed out releasing the fragrant cloud of sandalwood incense smoke. He took a paper from the woman and led me into the room where the air was warm and thick and filled with golden light. I saw Maharishi seated in a chair on a raised dais against one wall. Rows of course participants stood at tables facing him while they performed the puja. I was led up a center aisle and dropped off at a table in the second row, directly in front of Maharishi. The secretary whispered, "You can start the puja now," and walked away. On the table in front of me there was a lighted candle, a stick of burning sandalwood incense, camphor, fruit, and flowers. Although we had been practicing the puja daily, this time it reminded me of standing with Kenny Edwards during my initiation. I picked up the flowers and began reciting the Sanskrit words of the puja and finished by kneeling and bowing to Guru Dev. The secretary returned on cue and walked me onto Maharishi's dais motioning me into the chair beside him.

Maharishi looked at the paper the secretary handed him and leaned towards me. At that moment, I melted into a pool of bliss. His face was so close to mine that I couldn't focus on him. He whispered in his usual way of making statements sound like questions. "So, you accomplished the course work? You did well?" I heard his words as if from a distance. I noticed the color and softness of his translucent skin. It was as if he was there and not there at the same time. I watched his lips move, but I *felt* what he was saying more than heard it. His words felt like they were being transmitted from a place deep within him to a place deep within me. And the "me" was no longer me. It was my cosmic Self on the outside looking in. I had transcended the room and dived into an infinite pool of Being. Somewhere on the surface I heard Maharishi say, "So you will be a teacher now?" He could've been saying anything. "Cows are blue and the sky is pink, yes?" It wasn't as if I had to answer. I felt again that it was a one-sided transmission. What was taking place had nothing to do with understanding because I was barely capable of coherent thought. I was hearing his words as if they were coming through a tunnel. They passed through me, and God only knew where they were coming from and going to. I felt totally open and transparent as if I was nothing but Pure Consciousness. And bliss.

Next, Maharishi's voice took on a rhythmic cadence as if he was reciting a poem. It took a moment before I caught on—he was imparting the mantras for teaching Transcendental Meditation. He repeated them a few times before I realized I was supposed to repeat them back. I repeated them two or three more times until he was satisfied that I was pronouncing them correctly. He gave me some words of encouragement that I hardly heard, and then his secretary appeared and swooped me away. I floated down the aisle to the doors and left the room feeling I would never again be the same. Maharishi's presence had been so strong in me that

I felt like the cells in my body had been transformed.

The secretary dropped me in the hallway, the glass door closed behind me, and there I was in the world again, feeling as high as I had on the sidewalk on Gayley Avenue after my initiation. I paused in front of the young woman at the desk as if to ask, "Am I done?" She nodded then looked up at me with a smile that glowed even brighter than before. Later that day, the same woman startled me when she stopped me in the lunch line looking as if she had an important message to deliver. I wondered if there had been some mistake after all. I gazed into her sparkling eyes waiting for the news.

"You needn't worry. I just thought you might like to know this," she said, smiling. When you went into the room to see Maharishi this morning, there was a guardian angel with you. When you came out, there were six." I had no feeling of angels hovering around me but, on the other hand, I had no reason not to believe.

There were only a few days remaining in the course, which made the evening meetings with Maharishi all the more precious. Now that the hard work had been done everyone, including Maharishi, seemed relieved and freer. He was more open to talking about anything on anyone's mind. There was an outgoing man in his 30's who had become a course favorite whenever he stepped up to the microphone. The man was from a Black ghetto in Chicago and was known for keeping things real. Maharishi smiled. The man's question was about the abstaining from drugs for two weeks before starting TM. He said the rule would prevent anyone in his neighborhood from learning TM.

"Maharishi," he said, "there's no way the brothers can stay clean for two weeks."

Maharishi asked, "How did you do it?"

The man answered, "I lied."

Maharishi burst into laughter and said, "Then teach them to lie."

Smiling inwardly, I knew it had worked for me. I felt vindicated.

More than anything, I loved hearing Maharishi talk about God. Even as a young boy I had searched for God. As a young man when I was in Vietnam, where we'd go to sleep at night thinking we might not wake up in the morning, my need to find God was urgent. More than anything, I struggled to know why some good men died when bad guys survived. There was so much that happened in the war that didn't make sense.

I was elated to hear someone ask, "Maharishi, who are we to God?"

Maharishi answered, "We are the projection of a thought of God. Like a projection on a screen."

I was thrilled to hear him speak in detail. He said, "God is the impulse of the Absolute. The Absolute itself is nonfunctional. Its functional aspect is God—to create, to manifest. The Absolute is non-variable but the other side of its character is to be active, to create. The essential characteristic of God is to create. But where does God bring his material to create? The absolute is inactive. But inherent in inactivity is the ability to be active. Finite and infinite must be held together, like positive and negative poles. We call this the neutral point. Neither finite nor infinite holds them together. From this emerges all creation at once. God is attributed to be a judge because a judge is a neutral point. One must balance the Relative (the manifest universe) and the Unmanifest (the Absolute Field of Pure Consciousness) in awareness, to comprehend what God is."

I scribbled Maharishi's words in my notebook as quickly as he uttered them. For the first time, I was hearing the answer to my question. And he was answering it in detail. Also, for the first time, I was not being fed an "idea" about God as a personification, but I was hearing what God actually is.

"The omniscient nature of God is in the neutrality of life. Like a magnet, it maintains positive and negative poles and yet is a magnet. Although the two poles are totally opposed, the magnet holds them together."

I smiled inside listening to him define what for years—probably lifetimes—I'd longed to know.

"God doesn't do anything yet accomplishes everything. God is the balancing point, the neutral point, not affecting either of the two values in our awareness, yet maintaining both values in awareness. Just by being, the neutral point maintains the positive and negative.

"The Absolute and the finest manifestations of the Relative... God is neither of these. These two together are the products of a third thing. This can be called God. The analysis can go no further. When Consciousness is going from God Consciousness to Unity Consciousness, it can comprehend this. That something beyond which there is no possibility of anything more—is God.

"Being persons of God is not based on blind faith but on the enormous dignity of our state of consciousness."

So beautiful, I thought. *"The enormous dignity of our state of consciousness."* That was the key. In order to understand the reality of consciousness we had to be fully conscious. We had to know ourselves before we could know God.

On one of the final nights of teacher training, everyone was surprised when dozens of tour buses started to fill the narrow streets of La Antilla. A rumor spread that they had come to take us on an excursion to the Guadiana River that forms the border between Spain and Portugal.

The drive took several hours and it was dark by the time the buses let us off at a dock by the river. We boarded large tourist boats that took us slowly upstream floating somewhere between the starry sky above and its reflection in the water below. If others felt the same way I did, they were feeling profound satisfaction at being entrusted with the ancient knowledge of the Holy Tradition passed down to us through Guru Dev and then Maharishi. We were armed warriors ready for battle and now part of a collective destiny bigger than ourselves. Who could not feel expanded and joyous being in this amazing setting?

Standing outside on the deck of the ship, I felt permeated by bliss. I realized that within this expanded awareness all the constrictions and emotional drama that made up the personality named Tony Anthony, were gone—swallowed up by the Great Beyond. Even the demanding questions brought about by the war—a war that now seemed far away in a distant past—had been dissolved. Since there were no questions there was no need for answers.

Ah-hah—that was it! Once again, I realized the cosmic state Maharishi described in so many different ways was beyond the mind. The mind, for all its trying, for all its accumulation of knowledge, was rendered useless. The mind with all its thoughts could flail like a fish in the water but could grasp nothing. It was helpless here in this place that was no place at all. Here, I was free. Here was where I was made up of nothing but Pure Consciousness.

I realized that with this trip Maharishi was presenting us with a gift by allowing us a glimpse into his expanded state of consciousness. This trip to the Guadiana was not just some frivolous sightseeing tour. Everything Maharishi did was to expand our consciousness, and this was one more wonderful example. This was the reality of what he'd been saying all along. Now he was showing us what enlightenment is like.

Maharishi was sending us off back to the world with this incredible gift. He had found the perfect setting for his newly minted teachers to embark on our own adventures of discovery. Just downstream from where we were, where the Guadiana flowed into the Gulf of Cadiz, was the place where Columbus set sail on his journey where he discovered the New World. Where he found the world was not flat, but round. I was quietly overcome by a continually breaking wave of bliss washing over me. As we floated up-river beneath the infinite sky, Maharishi's quiet voice came over the speakers inspiring us to do great things, assuring us that we had been entrusted with the most important job on Earth. My heart surrendered ever more deeply to him.

The morning the course ended, the excitement was bittersweet. We were now teachers happy about being pushed out to enlighten the world, but sad about leaving the presence of our beloved master. I awakened early, having already packed my grandfather's hand-me-down leather suitcase the night before. After breakfast, I went for one last walk on the beach, strolling in my usual direction—east, towards the city of Huelva with its high-rise hotels visible in the distance. I had to step around the trash that had washed up on the sand—an inordinate collection of plastic bottles, bags, and bottle caps. It annoyed me to think about how we humans disrespect Mother Nature, and I felt good about being part of the solution to help put an end to this behavior. As Maharishi said, the answer is to raise people's consciousness. "Capture the fort. And win all the surrounding territory." I sat down on the sand beside a brightly painted red, yellow, and green fishing boat resting upside down on two logs. I felt something in my back pocket, leaned to the side and pulled it out. It was a folded piece of paper someone had handed me a few days before that I hadn't yet read. As it opened, I saw it was a single paragraph—a quote from Maharishi printed in blue ink.

Winter 1971/72

MAHARISHI, AT KASSEN, SEPTEMBER, 1971

"Naturalness is the basis of effectiveness. If one poses to be something else, one loses the charm of naturalness. The result is that one accumulates stress. We do not think of life—we live it. We do not think of ourselves too much. We do not think of others too much. We just behave in a natural way. Don't make moods—wonder what anyone thinks of us. We do not live life on the remarks of others. It is enough that we are naturally helpful to others. What others think of us is not our concern—it is their concern. If we are weak, we will always put ourselves at the whim of others. We do not base our lives on the opinions of others. But if we are not clear in our conscience then we will always be weak and will always mind the looks and remarks of other people. It is the weakness of individuality if it always looks to others. It is important only that we radiate life. Every individual must be a joy to himself, to his family and to his society."

A high-pitched yell came from down the beach. "The buses are here" and, just like that, my time in Antilla was over. I was officially a teacher of Transcendental Meditation. And I had no idea what my next step would be.

Maharishi Creates a University

eturning to the United States from teacher training wasn't as big a leap as returning from Vietnam, but still, my arrival had the flavor of coming from an unreal world back to a real one. In another way, it was just the opposite. I was back in the world, but no longer overwhelmed by it. This felt neither good nor bad—simply the way things were.

While I was in Spain my parents had rented out their home in Connecticut and moved to Savannah, Georgia, where my mother was fulfilling her dream of opening a pottery studio. My sister, Pati, along with her new husband and their daughter, had joined them helping to convert an old cotton warehouse on Savannah Harbor into a functioning pottery and retail shop. I showed up ostensibly to help with the shop, but mostly filled with the zealous fervor for teaching meditation. Although I had never intended to make teaching a career I was invigorated by my newfound knowledge and training, ready to see for myself if TM worked on others as it had for me.

Maharishi had suggested to new teachers that they line up family members and tell them they needed to practice teaching. My eighty-six-year-old grandmother was my first student and turned out to be my simplest to convince. Even before she was taught, she stood beside me at the puja table with tears of joy running down her cheeks. My cousin Cathy, who was my age, and her husband, an architect, grilled me with questions following the lecture, which made me dig deep into what I had learned in La Antilla. My conversations with them convinced me that I had learned the knowledge, and along with that, came the confidence I needed. In the end, they were convinced and from the moment they were initiated they loved meditating.

I stayed in Savannah just long enough to design a logo for the business, paint it on a sign above the door, and attend the opening of River Street Pottery. It felt wonderful to see my mother so fulfilled as at the opening. I'd never seen her so happy. Of course, it also may have had something to do with her being a newly-minted meditator.

Through the TM grapevine, I heard that Maharishi was in the process of creating a college in California. I didn't have to think about whether or not to go, I felt Maharishi calling me. Excited and enthusiastic, I headed west for the birth of Maharishi International University in Santa Barbara. I had a strong karmic connection with the place and I knew I would be comfortable there. As soon as I arrived, I remembered that the town was built on a slice of paradise. More than ever, I appreciated being in Santa Barbara, which embodied California's incredible natural beauty—mountains, sea, and wide-open sky.

MIU was located in Isla Vista, a suburb twenty minutes away from the center of town. Isla Vista had a vibe all its own. It was home almost exclusively to University of California at Santa Barbara students and teachers, which at the time, meant hippies. However, the area's once revolutionary fervor had mellowed into more of a weed and surfer vibe. The college was housed in an apartment complex named Casa Royale, a three-story, white-stucco, rectangular apartment complex built around a center courtyard with a pool, a few funky palms and a scrubby lawn. MIU rented one end, which included a large dining room/kitchen and about a third of the apartments. The remaining two-thirds housed students who were like students at any California school, partying on weekends and smoking weed whenever. We, the MIU staff, dressed in our businesslike suit-and-ties and skirt-and-jackets were the impossibly straight ones, but given the hang-loose vibe, we all got along famously.

Being part of the fledgling university meant experiencing Maharishi's Movement in a novel way. MIU was like a foreign outpost, a kind of government embassy in a distant land, far removed from the seat of government, its leader and his headquarters.

My art background fit into this project immediately. Professors were just beginning to videotape courses and graphic designers were needed to produce the charts and graphs. There were about twenty staff by the time I arrived including a dozen professors under the guidance of MIU President Keith Wallace: Michael Weinless, David and Rhoda Orme-Johnson, Michael and Charlotte Caine, Larry Domash, Frank Peppentin, and others. Besides the teachers and the first group of students, there were kitchen staff, housecleaners, maintenance people and other volunteers to help the place run. When the original head of the graphics department left abruptly, I found myself in charge. Lindsey Shoemaker, Jeffrey Glasser, Gail Metropole and I worked in what was actually a bedroom on the ground floor. Our role was to produce visuals for the courses to illustrate the concepts being discussed. This was in the days before computer design. Graphics were done on mat board, illustrations done with colored pens, and text produced by hand with rub-on wax letters.

I interacted with the video crew—Michael Ritter, Flash Pflaumer and Duke Gibbs—three creative geniuses who had transformed a portion of the kitchen and dining room into a working television studio. With three cameras wheeled around on a not-quite-smooth greenish-brown linoleum floor, the professors pointed at our graphics propped on three-legged easels. The methods may have been crude, but they helped infuse every subject with Maharishi's knowledge. Maharishi International University was off and running.

I enjoyed being in the company of meditators with a shared practice and purpose. It made working together seamless, without egos and an absence of rancor and hassles. Life was happy and healthful. We ate fresh organic vegetables grown by a commune in the hills called Sunburst Farm, founded by a disciple of Paramahansa Yogananda, a famous Indian guru who taught meditation and yoga in America from the 1930s to the 1950s. It was fun comparing notes with the members who delivered the produce and did a different type of meditation and dressed more like hippies than business folks.

Aside from the usual course offerings such as math and science, etc., Maharishi asked a few trusted people from other fields to create courses. Walter Koch, who was an early follower of Maharishi's and rumored to be in Cosmic Consciousness, was one. He was a retired aeronautical engineer with a shock of snow-white hair. He showed up one morning in our small studio, attempting to explain the video he wanted to make. His thinking was as fluid and as hard to pin down as water in a stream. But after days of back-and-forth, trial and error, we finally succeeded in making his abstract concepts concrete. Given the Stone-Age technology we employed, the course videos turned out quite well. But more important, they helped fulfill Maharishi's desire for a functioning university based on his principles of Creative Intelligence.

Although Isla Vista was part of wealthy and conservative Santa Barbara, it had its own free-wheeling attitude. We meditators, who tended to be quite focused and serious, eventually acclimated somewhat by joining in nude swimming at the nearby clothing-optional beach. Alas, our fun was short-lived when we got word that Maharishi wanted to move MIU to a place with less distractions. As much as we enjoyed our relaxed lifestyle, Maharishi's thinking made sense. Isla Vista wasn't exactly suited as a place for a university founded on the ancient traditions of the Vedas. Regardless, we were all shocked when Keith relayed the news that MIU was going to move to an existing college campus the TM Movement had purchased in Fairfield, Iowa. The thought of moving to the cornfields of the Midwest didn't sit well with many of us. We suggested more appealing alternatives, but to no avail. Maharishi, of course, prevailed.

But the location of MIU wasn't important to me. My goal, always, was to be near Maharishi. His headquarters were in Seelisberg, Switzerland.

There was no way I could see to get there. But I could get one step closer.

Becoming a Devotee

Compelled by my desire to be near Maharishi, I signed up for a six-month-long rounding course in Interlaken, Switzerland. In no time, I was placing the contents of my grandfather's heavy leather suitcase into an antique dresser in a high-ceilinged room in the palatial Victoria-Jungfrau Hotel. A well-preserved remnant of another era, the hotel was the centerpiece of a valley between two lakes, the Thun and Brienz. There were sumptuous linens and a huge down comforter on the bed and a hand-loomed wool rug on the parquet floor—and then there was the view. The balcony faced the snow-capped Jungfrau, one of the most photographed mountains in Switzerland. Given the setting as well as our accommodations, it could be said that the subtext for the course was sumptuousness, which made our day-long schedule of rounding ridiculously comfortable. I performed my yoga asanas on the comforter spread out on the wool rug. We took prescribed breaks, walk-and-talks, easy half hour strolls with a friend or two, to integrate the deep silence of meditation into activity. These walks in town took us past the windows of high-end shops displaying designer clothes, Italian shoes, and antiques.

One store, specialized in deep red, Mediterranean coral jewelry, a coral rumored to nourish the heart. Because Maharishi wore a strand of these beads, course participants snapped them up. According to tradition, masters "blessed" beads worn by their disciples. So, each time Maharishi visited Interlaken, some of the group placed their beads on his coffee table, and during his talks, he would pick up a strand or two for a few seconds, and then put them down. A mountain of beads ensued. Finally, as Maharishi stepped up onto his dais one day, he glanced at the untenable pile of beads and asked all the owners to come up and retrieve their strands. As he watched the procession of people sheepishly gathering up their beads, he told them with a laugh, "You do more for the beads than the beads do for you."

The bead craze was a perfect example of how Maharishi subdued various obsessions that popped up from time to time. These could be about anything, but were usually about diet. The expanding state of consciousness created by rounding seemed to unleash the mind, freeing it from its usual ways of thinking. This openness created a fertile ground for rumors to run rampant among participants. Someone overhearing the benefits of a certain type of diet could change everyone's eating habits within a matter of days—even without talking about what they heard.

After a while I became bored with the daily routine of

rounding. As I once heard Maharishi say, when you're sitting in a hot bath, after a while, the water no longer feels hot, so to feel the heat again, you have to stir it up. During a long stretch of foggy days, I felt like stirring things up. I found a trail behind the hotel leading up a mountain called the Harder Kulm. It was considered to be a minor ascent in comparison to the giants like the Jungfrau, because it could be climbed without technical skills. Although I knew it was impossible to judge the degree of difficulty from the perspective of standing at the base, it looked to be a fairly easy trek up a hill. Mountain climbing is the antithesis of rounding, the goal of which is to allow the body to settle into deep rest. Meditation lowers the metabolic rate, and rounding, since we were meditating for most of the day, slows the metabolism so much that, at times, it's a monumental effort just to walk from one's room to the dining room.

Nevertheless, once the idea became fixated in my mind, there was no ignoring it. One morning after completing a single round, I laced up my boots and set out. The trail was easy-going at first, without factoring in my slow metabolism. My enthusiasm overshadowed the reality that even our short walk-and-talks had proved tiring. But once on the trail, my adrenaline kicked in and carried me for a few hours until the terrain leveled out, and delivered me to the edge of a cliff. Sitting down to rest, I was astonished to find myself looking down on the tops of clouds. Fortunately, this satisfied me and tamped down the desire to climb farther. I was tired for days afterward. People had been asked to leave courses for such stupidity.

Watching videos of Maharishi as we did twice a day—afternoon, and evening—made my heart expand with love for him. Before falling asleep one night, I found myself considering the idea of becoming a devotee, although I had no real picture of what that entailed. On the grossest level (the most material level) I thought, what would be in it for me? I was embarrassed that I was capable of thinking in such a selfish way. But, since I wanted to get to the real truth, I thought I must pursue even the most selfish reason. And, the answer came quickly, and was actually a part of the question: "What was in it for me? *Nothing—nothing at all.*" It was a perfect response because it meant becoming a devotee would be a selfless pursuit, performing an action with no thought of gain or return. And that meant, acting out of love, unconditionally. On an even deeper level, it was total surrender, and the total surrender of the self means, dissolution of the ego. Without ego, what followed would be freedom.

Bingo! I laughed with my head resting on the pillow. I was sure I'd found the personal key to ending suffering: Without a "me" there would be no one left to suffer.

Ever since I saw Maharishi for the first time during the summer at Humboldt College, I felt a deep reverence for this holy man. It could be called love, because the desire to be with him, to follow him, was deeper than words can express. I wasn't sure where the love came from—perhaps from having been with him in past lifetimes? Whatever it was, it was real and a force that propelled me to act. The trouble was I had no idea how to go about it. The only hint came from observing others doing service. I had noticed some longtime members of Maharishi's staff rushing along hallways carrying armfuls of towels and cleaning supplies. I learned where Maharishi's rooms must be when I saw them using the elevator and stairways leading to the third-floor, guarded by the ever-stoic German guards that always seemed to be around. As I was checking things out one day, the woman, who I presumed to be in charge, passed me in the hallway. I seized the moment and stopped her, asking if there was some way I might help. Not knowing what to expect, I found her surprisingly friendly and accommodating. She immediately put me at ease as if what I was asking was the most normal thing in the world. Her name was Barbara Woods and she said, "Of course you can be of help." Without hesitating, she led us past the guards up the stairs to Maharishi's suite.

There was a flurry of activity in Maharishi's suite. Several of the people I'd seen working in the front meeting rooms were scurrying through the hallways here. Barbara led the way into the suite's large white-tiled bathroom, which to me looked perfectly clean. I assumed I was about to discover a whole new level of cleanliness. I was given a bucket of maintenance supplies, so I mixed some soap and water in the bucket and began scrubbing Maharishi's bathroom walls. As soon as I began, I felt at ease, and the longer I worked, the better I felt. I had done manual labor before, but this was different: the work was a product of love for an enlightened master, and more personally, for all he had given me. I felt my heart expanding; it felt like I was scrubbing my way to bliss.

This was what devotion was all about.

I knew the story of Totakacharya, a disciple of Shankara, the first great monk in Maharishi and Guru Dev's lineage. The disciple, originally called Giri, was not known for his intellect, but for his work ethic and his loyalty to the master. One day, while Giri was washing the master's clothes, Shankara delayed the day's lesson telling the other monks he would not start until Giri had finished with his chores. A learned monk pointed to a wall and told the master that teaching Giri would be like trying to teach a wall. But Shankara rewarded Giri for his loyalty and devotion by transmitting the complete knowledge of all the śāstras (precepts) to him. When the enlightened Giri composed a Sanskrit poem in the totaka meter in praise of Shankara, he became known as "Totakacharya"

Maharishi was my Shankara.

Maharishi flew in by helicopter from Seelisberg to spend the day with us. At the end of the day when he was about to leave, he mentioned he was looking for a few people to work on staff in Seelisberg. I found it interesting that he mentioned it himself because he usually left such practical matters to one of his secretaries or course leaders. His announcement seemed like a personal request. He finished by asking, specifically, if there was anyone who had experience in advertising.

The word "advertising" got my attention. I had grown up learning everything there was to know about advertising. I was the son of Al Anthony, a Madison Avenue whiz kid. When I was growing up, my father's big accounts—Fiat, Scandinavian Airlines and Revlon—were the nightly topics of dinner conversation. He enjoyed telling my mother, sister and me every detail about his workday in New York. Soon, I knew how to create an ad campaign—how the creative director sketched his ideas for the ads, what the copywriter wrote, and how the art director combined the elements to create the finished product. My father loved taking me to work with him. He proudly introduced me to each member of the art department—the layout men, the illustrators, and the lettering man who hand-lettered each ad. I met the copywriters, who in contrast to the ebullient artists, were a dour lot. I also met the account executives who were responsible for delivering the finished product to the clients. Compared to everyone else, they were the most gregarious and out-going. I wasn't exactly sure how, but my father embodied all these people in their assorted roles. I was certain he would be comfortable doing everything by himself, and of course garnering all the glory. By the time I was a teenager, I knew the advertising business inside and out. My father always expected I would follow in his footsteps, in the business where he had been so successful.

So, when I heard Maharishi say the word "advertising," it felt as if he had shot an arrow at me. Although I was sitting far back in the sea of course participants, Maharishi's eyes managed to find mine, if only for a split-second. Even so, I didn't imagine he knew who I was amongst the hundreds in the audience. Not including when he had appeared in the guise of Hans in Santa Barbara, the only time we had met in the flesh was when he'd made me a teacher in La Antilla. Somehow, he had picked the perfect word to get my attention, and I couldn't deny the odd sensation of thinking he was speaking to me.

And yet, mostly because of my shyness, I denied it.

My mind struggled to make sense of how it was possible for him to know me so well—or even, at all. Since I believed he came to Santa Barbara to find me, why couldn't I accept that anything at all was possible? In the end, I admitted that this realm was beyond my capacity to know.

Meanwhile, dozens of people waved their hands in the air, like ships flying signal flags, trying to get Maharishi's attention. Obviously, it was a valuable prize to work in Seelisberg. Maharishi shook his head a little, perhaps not expecting such a vigorous response and asked those interested to meet with his secretary, a tall New Zealander named Gavon, outside the hall. Gavon would take down everyone's names and qualifications. I didn't raise my hand nor did I meet with Gavon, because I'd never seriously considered working for Maharishi. However, it didn't occur to me at the time that by cleaning his bathroom, I had already begun to work for him. Since cleaning the bathroom was done anonymously it felt different. It was a safe fantasy, as if I were acting the part of a devotee without facing the reality of what it might entail. It may also have been that I was only putting my toe in to test the waters before I was sure about taking the plunge. Maharishi left for Seelisberg the next day, presumably having performed his ablutions in his sparkling clean bathroom. The course returned to normal and I took my usual long walk with my sweet walk-and-talk partner, Peggy, chatting about everything under the sun.

At the afternoon meeting the following day, Maharishi's secretary Gavon made a surprise return appearance. He had come alone to announce that Maharishi had not yet found a suitable candidate for the advertising position among those who had applied. When he asked whether there might not be someone else with the qualifications, this time I was quite certain his question was pointed directly at me. As much as I tried to deny it, I knew Maharishi was calling me.

After the meeting, I found Gavon in the hallway. When I approached him and mentioned the advertising position, he had me write my name on a piece of paper and offhandedly tucked it into a notebook. And, that was all. At least until the next morning when someone knocked on my door with an urgent message from Maharishi. He wanted me to come to Seelisberg, immediately.

I hadn't really expected it to happen, so it came as a shock. There was the, *how did he know me?* aspect. But also, there was the very real and present shock of having to leave the subtle course atmosphere at the height of rounding. Now, weeks into the course, because of the intense schedule, we were incredibly spaced-out, and with our metabolisms slowed, we were barely able to function. I doubted my ability to travel when I could barely complete my prescribed walk-and-talk without frequent rest-stops. And I wondered how I was going to navigate across Switzerland. There was no mention of coming down from rounding slowly, simply Maharishi's message to come to Seelisberg, *immediately*.

As I stuffed my clothes into my grandfather's old leather suitcase, I felt the power of Maharishi's pull, which my mind and body translated into a kind of nervous anticipation, a wariness of the unknown. This should have been a clue that I had jumped from the spiritual frying pan into the fire.

And, that there was no turning back.

Into the Fire

I felt more than a little trepidation as I dragged my grandfather's heavy suitcase from my room down the hall to the elevator. I was departing early in the morning while people were still rounding without saying any goodbyes. Everyone who needed to, knew where I was going. I was operating so slowly that just making the downstairs trek to the dining room felt like a major expedition. It was difficult to leave the comfort of the Victoria Jungfrau Hotel. I was thankful to be alone in the dining room without having to explain what I wasn't sure of myself. I was having enough trouble coming to grips with making my way to Seelisberg, stepping out into the tough world of taxis and trains and even a steamer, I was told, to cross Lake Lucerne.

But as soon as I stopped worrying about what was ahead, I was fine. In fact, the subtle state of being that rounding creates made everything appear better and brighter than usual. The taxi ride along one of the lakes to the station let me appreciate a part of Interlaken I hadn't discovered. Standing on the station platform with weak knees, I was barely able to function physically, and yet everything around me was delightful. I felt like I had bought a ticket to heaven.

I was filled with wonder at everything around me.

Once I was on the train, with my suitcase as my comforting companion, I was more than happy—joyous, even. The train left the station slowly and seamlessly. No harsh jerks to get things moving—just, little by little, rolling up to speed, Swiss style. It felt good to be anonymous, unknown by anybody on the train. I was happy to be just another passenger watching the magical mountains out the window. I loved soaking in the musical sounds of foreign languages being spoken around me. That, together with the muted sound of the wheels on the tracks, pulled me into a soothing reverie. I was floating through the Swiss landscape with Maharishi's protective umbrella over me. I was amazed when we pulled into the Lucerne station after what seemed like only a few minutes' journey. Diving headlong into the bustling railroad station was a whole other level of fantasy. Hungry Swiss travelers stood at food stands dipping fat sausages into mustard between bites of hard rolls, while others scurried to and from trains—all part of the "Lila"—the joyous cosmic play of humankind.

I passed beneath the huge arch of the main entrance into still another reality. The air outside was heavy with humidity and smelled strongly of Lake Lucerne. Across a huge lawn, the dark blue lake stretched out into infinity. Tied to a dock was a beautiful white-hulled steamer with a black smokestack like an antique from a past lifetime. I wrestled my suitcase across the grass to a ticket booth to buy a ticket to Seelisberg. The woman frowned at me and said I needed a ticket for Treib, and from there I would take a train up the mountain. A ticket for that would have to be purchased separately in Treib.

I found a seat in an open-air restaurant on the stern of the steamer's main deck with an unobstructed view of the lake. As the boat pulled away from the dock, with a hot pot of tea and a pastry in front of me, I marveled at yet another Swiss reality, a line of grand hotels along the lakeshore regally lit for the evening hours. With swans riding the bow wave towards shore, we slid through the colorful reflections of the hotels painted on the surface of the water. Soon we were enveloped in the dark of the middle of the huge lake—a small sea surrounded by snow-capped mountains. The wind whipped a fine spray against the plexiglass barriers around the deck.

For the first time, I considered the honor of Maharishi's invitation to work for him. In spiritual terms, I'd been granted a grace. I had no idea of the job I was being hired for, but actually, having no expectation helped. For now, I would enjoy the enchantment of being on a steamer sliding across the surface of this inland sea. I would take each step, one at a time. With the sound of the engines lowering their pitch, we glided towards a dock along the shore.

In a marvel of Swiss-watch-like precision, the steamer nudged up against the dock without the slightest jolt. A deckhand jumped onto the dock while another lowered a gangplank in an effortless ballet performed for a lone disembarking passenger. The plank was raised, the deckhand jumped aboard, and we were off without a wasted second. I watched the process repeated at each village along the shore as the night grew darker. The farther we were from Lucerne, the more infrequent the stops. The closer we came to the other end of the lake, the more mysterious the surroundings. The mountains, now ominous black silhouettes barely indistinguishable from the sky, made me anxious. When Treib was announced as the next stop, I moved up to the bow of the steamer searching for the lights of a town. Instead, what emerged from the dark was a lone brown chalet. A familiar wave washed over me, my old childish fear of the unknown, and, for a moment, I was gripped by the thought of remaining on the steamer.

The pitch of the engines lowered and we slid closer to the empty dock. As I moved near the gangplank, I was aware of a few disapproving frowns from the few remaining passengers. I was reminded of the woman's unfriendly face in the ticket booth back in Lucerne when I asked for a ticket to Seelisberg. As I learned later, residents of Seelisberg were known as "Ru's," short for "guru," an unkind nickname for Maharishi's followers. An Indian guru with hundreds of followers in residence did not fit in with the reserved Swiss concept of what is acceptable.

I was the only one disembarking at Treib. The boat nudged against the dock, the gangplank was lowered, and I walked the plank like I was being forced off a pirate ship. Watching the steamer pull away, I was left alone on the dock without another human in sight until I spotted the funicular to Seelisberg. A light in a single train car on a platform was angled uphill with a lone man in uniform sitting in the dim light of the car. I approached and he sold me a ticket and motioned me into a seat. Although the car was angled at the slope of the mountain, the seats were level. Once the car was set in motion, we were swept silently and effortlessly through the dark up the mountain. The end of our journey was an empty parking lot. The conductor pointed to a road that disappeared uphill into the dark. "Maharishi" he said.

I had come this far, so there was no turning back. I was tired then, and all I could think of was finding a bed. Grandfather's suitcase had mysteriously gained weight, so I hefted it onto my shoulders and headed up the mountain road. For the first mile or so there was nothing but forest until the road grew steeper and cut through a rock cliff. Without streetlights, the darkness permeated everything except a ceiling of stars. In the cold air, the dampness from the lake crept over me even from far below.

This was not how I pictured arriving in Seelisberg.

Welcome to Heaven

I followed the road in darkness. After at least an hour of walking, I reached the outskirts of a village I hoped was Seelisberg. I passed a tiny chapel and a small inn dimly lit by a streetlight and then the road leveled out into what appeared to be the center of town. Two large buildings that looked like hotels materialized out of the dark. They faced each other from opposite sides of the street, connected by a covered footbridge. There were no signs to identify them, but I hoped that at least one was Maharishi's headquarters because I was too exhausted to walk any further. The building to the lakeside was squeezed between the road and the edge of a cliff. The lake, somewhere far below, couldn't be seen although its presence could still be felt. The only light came from behind a pair of double doors on the ground level of the larger of the two buildings. Through the glass doors, I was heartened to see a young man seated behind a desk, dressed in a dark suit jacket and tie, which somehow told me he belonged in the Movement. When I opened the door and emerged from the dark, he sat up straight in surprise and eyed me warily.

"Is this Maharishi's headquarters?" I asked, and he nodded.

"Maharishi asked me to come," I told him.

"Maharishi *is not here*," he answered in a strong German accent, "He is down on the lake."

At a loss, I asked if there was a place where I could sleep. He told me I could take any room that was empty in the Kulm. He sent me up the stairs behind him, told me to take a left turn and take the bridge across the street.

It now became even more obvious that I hadn't really known what to expect in coming here. I had simply been following instructions but now that I was here, I wondered if Maharishi would even remember he had asked me to come. I was exhausted enough not to worry about "what-ifs." For now, I would be satisfied to find a pillow on which to lay my head.

I dragged Grandfather's suitcase up the stairs, across the covered walkway, into the quiet, frigid Hotel Kulm. Heading down a dark hall, I knocked on each door worried that I might be waking someone. If I knocked and heard nothing, I opened the door and turned on the light, but in every room, there was either a towel hanging by a sink, a shirt hung out to dry or rumpled sheets and blankets on the bed. It wasn't until I took the stairs up to the next floor that I found an empty room. A dim yellow glow from a ceiling fixture revealed a single bed with a bare mattress, and a pillow. There were no signs of life—no clothing or towels or anything—so I claimed the empty space. I was exhausted but satisfied; a mattress was all I needed. I closed the door, stripped to my underwear, and flopped down on the mattress pulling my wool coat over me. In the moments before falling asleep, I remembered a time in the army when I arrived at Fort Jackson, South Carolina for infantry training in the middle of the night and had to search a barracks for an empty cot. That room was filled with twenty snoring soldiers. There were no snoring soldiers here, and no one awakened me during the night complaining I had stolen his cot. In the coming days, I found a wool blanket, sheets, a pillowcase, and a towel and declared the room my own. My new quarters didn't equal my room in the Victoria-Jungfrau, but my heart warmed knowing I was in Maharishi's home.

The next day, I woke up early because I was in a new place and wanted to explore my surroundings. It was too early for breakfast—Movement kitchens always served meals after meditation time. So, I did my pranayama then sunk into meditation. The first few minutes of meditation were spent reviewing the day before—the endless impressions of the Swiss countryside appearing in the train window, the lakes, the rivers, the mountains—but, sinking deeper, I became aware of my current whereabouts. Although I hadn't yet seen Seelisberg in the light of day, I knew I had landed somewhere like no place I had ever been. There existed an abiding quietness—an abiding *silence,* really. After all, this is where Maharishi lived. Being on courses had given me a taste of his powerful presence, but this was where he actually *lived.* I had read in Yogananda's *Autobiography of a Yogi* and other books of ashrams in India, that the powerful energy of the resident saint could be felt for miles. I couldn't be certain yet that this was the reality, but I was becoming more and more certain that I wasn't sure of anything anymore. More things were happening that *didn't* make sense than things that *did*. Whether I liked it or not, I was opening up to a force much greater and more powerful than I could have imagined. I had an innate sense that everything would be taken care of if I just let go and let things happen.

At first, I found it difficult to meditate because my mind wanted me to dress and bolt out the door, to explore this new world. But the deep, steadfast silence kept me inward in a way I had not yet experienced. The silence had a hold on me that kept me in meditation making me unable to open my eyes and dive into the day. My eyelids remained bolted shut. This was a battle—a war between the mind and the silence. Although the mind, filled with its usual endless stream of thoughts, emotions and desires, demanded action, it was the deep silence that won out. It settled inside me and around me until I was completely saturated. I felt myself expanding into its infinity, growing ever deeper, ever richer and more awake. It was an impossible silence—one that was so still and unmoving, that it was its own field of existence. It was impossibly deep, yet rich, vibrant and alive, filled with color and energy. *Impossible.* Yet true.

When I opened my eyes two hours had passed and I was worried I had missed breakfast. I threw some water on my face, brushed my teeth, shaved in the sink in my room, and rushed down the hall to the stairs and found the dining room on the first floor of the hotel. The spacious room had floor-to-ceiling windows facing a spectacular view of the lake and a single imposing mountain on the far shore. Breakfast was in high gear.

The room was filled and buzzing with energy. It appeared that most of the staff was present. The meal was exactly the same as on the course in Interlaken: muesli, granola, yogurt, bananas, oranges, and peppermint tea. During the course, people ate in silence and the atmosphere was inward and subdued, but here the air was vibrant and energetic with people chatting away in different languages. I heard German and what sounded like a Scandinavian tongue and was relieved when I found a table of English speakers. As I took an empty seat at the table, I was thankful to be among friendly Englishmen who politely introduced themselves. And, as it turned out, they were graphic designers. When I explained that Maharishi had summoned me to Seelisberg, presumably, to work on advertising, they had no idea what that might entail. There was no advertising staff as far as any of them knew. One suggested that I hang out until I received instructions from Maharishi. They all chuckled when I asked them how Maharishi would know I was there, and one of them said, "He knows." I was left with the impression that there was no specific chain of command to reach Maharishi and no pressing need to reach him either. I was happy to let go of trying and let everything unfold in its own time.

With nothing urgent, I explored the tiny village of Seelisberg. It was a clear and brisk morning and the pleasant bucolic aroma of grass and cows was in the air. In the daylight I saw that Maharishi's headquarters consisted of two large hotels connected by a bridge, the Kulm and the Sonnenberg, as well as a few ancillary buildings. In addition to the Waldhaus Inn and the small Sonnenberg chapel, the remainder of the village was a combination of forested hills and well-tended dairy farms with dark wood barns and traditional painted Swiss chalets. Up the road there was a single tiny grocery store with sundries and a large selection of chocolate. Quiet and unspoiled, the village was overwhelmed by natural beauty. Forests and meadows above the town spilled down the side of a mountain coming to an abrupt halt at a sheer cliff above Lake Lucerne, at least a thousand feet below. From across the lake a huge triangular mountain gazed at Seelisberg as if it were keeping watch over the village.

Seelisberg is in the state of Uri, "the forest canton," the least inhabited in Switzerland. It is where the Swiss come to rejuvenate, climbing and hiking in these gorgeous surroundings. Not far from the hotels, trails wound through a pine forest that followed the ridge. Other trails snaked their way downhill to Rutli, the birthplace of Switzerland, which was a lone meadow with a plaque honoring the place where William Tell, the Swiss folk hero, shot an apple off his son's head with an arrow.

I took a trail behind the Hotel Sonnenberg that circled around the side of the mountain and emerged at an overlook. There a perfectly positioned wooden bench offered a breathtaking view of the lake. The steamers, appearing no longer than an inch, drew white lines on the lake's dark blue surface with their wakes. Tiny automobiles skimmed along the road bordering the far shore. The view from the bench gave me the feeling that Seelisberg was insulated and untouched. From up there, the world looked like a miniature train set, moving at a simple, steady pace.

I wondered if Maharishi had picked Seelisberg for his headquarters for just this reason. Viewing the world in miniature from high up, it would be easy to fashion it exactly as he pleased.

Interview in the Dark

After being in Seelisberg for almost a week, I was approached in the dining room one night by Bob Roth, who was in charge of Maharishi's public relations and one of his most visible staff. Bob, tall and thin, vibrated enough energy to light a city. He introduced himself and delivered a message from Maharishi, that he was aware I had arrived. I told him I had been wondering whether Maharishi knew I was here.

"Maharishi knows everything that goes on around here," Bob said with a twinkle in his eye.

The next evening, I was eating alone in the dining room when Bob arrived breathless beside my table. "Maharishi wants to see you," he said.

When I didn't jump to my feet instantly, he added, "Now."

I barely kept up with Bob as he raced upstairs and across

the bridge to the Sonnenberg. We entered a dark hallway where a group of people stood reverently outside a set of glass double doors covered by sheets. The group made way for us, knowing we had been summoned by Maharishi.

Bob tapped gently on the glass and we heard Maharishi's voice. "Yes?"

My heart pounded in anticipation of being alone in a room with Maharishi. Bob nudged the door open slightly, poked his head inside and announced, "Maharishi, Tony Anthony is here to see you."

The words echoed in my brain. Our two names in the same sentence. Maharishi and Tony Anthony.

My thoughts raced like a runaway freight train with boxcars filled with idiotic thoughts. Did Maharishi know I was the one who cleaned his bathroom? Is that why I'm here? Does he remember when he came for me in Santa Barbara disguised as Hans Sebbelov? Was that really him? Should I ask?

Hearing Maharishi's voice, brought the train of thoughts to a halt. "Yes, yes. Tell him to come in." He sounded happy, as if seeing me was the most exciting thing that could be happening at that moment.

Bob pushed the door open wide enough for me to see, although there was only pitch black in front of me. Since the hall was dark as well, I couldn't see Maharishi at all.

His voice came from the dark. "Yes, come."

Bob gently urged me forward with a hand on my back and whispered in my ear, "Sit down right where you are standing.

Maharishi is in front of you."

This may have been the case, but since I couldn't see a thing I wasn't sure of Maharishi's exact location and was anxious about running into him.

Bob left, closing the door behind him and the darkness became even more blinding. In Vietnam, it was a necessary survival skill to become expert at seeing in the dark. But here my expertise was useless. There are different degrees of darkness at night. Darkness with stars and darkness without stars. And then there's darkness in a cave. This was like that. So I lowered myself in place crossing my legs on a rug and, finally, through the darkness, I felt Maharishi's presence. It was like a patch of softness within the dark. *Softness imbued with power.*

We sat in silence until I heard a soft, "Yes?" The sound of his voice came from an arm's length in front of me and at the same level, so he was also seated on the floor. I was aware of the room being very warm. It was like sitting in front of a warm fire on a cold winter's night.

I had no idea of what to say. I could hardly think at all. I felt as if I was swimming underwater in a deep, even boundless, ocean. I heard my mind conjure up a thought, something like "I'm Tony Anthony, Maharishi. I was told you wanted to see me." But the thought left as quickly as it came. Whatever words I heard in my head sounded odd and empty, not important enough to be spoken out loud.

I was aware of my presence in the middle of a field of empty space. And I knew that whatever I was thinking or feeling, was happening beyond me, or outside of me—actually, both inside and out at the same time—in a void, infinitely large in every direction.

In this deep emptiness around me—and around Maharishi as well—it seemed like we were both floating somewhere in this spaceless space. I fell helplessly in thrall of this place that was a non-place, this space that was no-space, where I was both nowhere, and yet everywhere, all at once. And, strange as it might seem, wherever I was and was not, everything was okay. Not only that, it felt familiar to me as if I had been there before—or maybe I was always there, but didn't know it.

Perhaps this was what pure Being felt like.

Perhaps this *was* pure Being. Maybe so, but it didn't want to be named.

And then I realized I was having trouble locating myself within this unbounded field. Certainly, there was no physical me. That part had melted away and become part of the infinite field of Being. In fact, that's what I was. That's *all* I was.

Sometime later, long after this meeting, I was on an advanced course and heard Maharishi say, "we are not individuals, we are cosmic." I was instantly brought back to this moment with Maharishi in the dark. I knew what he meant because, as we sat there together, he had shown me. And, I was certain of what I wanted, which was nothing less than becoming part of pure Being or pure Consciousness—two phrases that aim at defining the undefinable from perhaps slightly different angles.

In the darkness, Maharishi asked me some simple questions—

which, after what he had just shown me, seemed superfluous. Where was I born and where did I grow up? He asked about my family. "Do you have a brother or sister? Where do you live? What was your education? Tell me about your mother and your father."

I had no idea about the importance of defining myself in such ways that seemed like creating simple sketches against an infinite background. Or, maybe that *was* the idea—to create a recognizable picture of an individual suspended in infinity.

But, really, I had no clue.

He seemed particularly interested in my father and what he did for a living. When I answered, I noticed that I was hyper-aware of myself speaking. I both heard and saw words come out of my mouth as if they were in a cartoon bubble.

But who was this person speaking? I asked of myself. I seemed to be creating both the person I was and what I was saying out of nothing as I spoke.

It seemed almost as if I was in an echo chamber. As I was seeing and hearing myself speak, I looked at myself from *outside* myself. I heard myself calling my father *an advertising genius*. Then I recalled that advertising was the reason Maharishi had me come to Seelisberg.

After that, I can't remember much more. In the end, I sensed that he knew the answers to whatever questions he was asking, so in one way, it seemed as if his questions were superfluous yet, I knew there had to be a reason he was asking. Perhaps to localize his unbounded consciousness. But that was just one more thing that was "beyond me." And, of course, this was my first real meeting alone with Maharishi, so I hardly knew what to expect. In the years to come, I'd learn that there is really no knowing an enlightened being or their thinking. They live and act in an infinite field, which to the unenlightened is not even imaginable.

At some point I lost all awareness of where I was and what was happening and remained in that space beyond the mind where the individual didn't exist. I have no idea how long we talked; it may have been a few minutes or a few hours. I am certain that much more was said, but if asked how I knew, even that much, I couldn't say. I am quite certain we had a long in-depth conversation that was not a spoken one, and yet everything was completely understood. Thinking back on it, had Maharishi used words, what he conveyed would have taken years, perhaps even lifetimes.

I am absolutely positive that this transmission—or whatever it can be called—took place, because for days and weeks and even years afterward, at surprisingly odd times, I have recalled specific information that was conveyed without any recollection of having heard it through my ears. I've tried to explain this but cannot. It is just one more thing that can't be understood by the thinking mind. My recollection of this mysterious conversation emerges from time to time, but since it took place on a subtler level of existence, pieces sometimes show up as "ah-ha!" realizations during particularly silent moments where pure Consciousness has overtaken activity, but on the surface of life the conversation remains only a vague memory.

During the session in the dark, I had the sense that Maharishi made some necessary repairs for my well-being. I say this because afterward, I felt as if a gap in my evolution was closed, as if obstacles that had previously been holding me back, were gone. Since I am speaking about a very subtle, very abstract area, I can't explain what the obstacles were, but I do know that in the coming days, I felt freer, lighter and infinitely more powerful. Everything I did felt easier—even effortless.

As a confirmation that a shift in me had occurred, I noticed that others treated me differently. Prior to the interview, I was still an outsider. Afterward, I fit in. Others on staff respected me as if my standing was elevated, and they now considered me an equal. I was accepted as one of Maharishi's close devotees. It was as if everybody suddenly knew I'd been given an access pass to an exclusive club. I guessed that Maharishi had handed me a protective umbrella like the one the others carried.

Sometime after the meeting, Bob Roth told me that he was amazed at how quickly Maharishi had brought me into his inner circle. Bob admitted that it had taken him years to gain the kind of access Maharishi had afforded me in such a short time.

I've never understood why I deserved this honor.

Designing a Life

ollowing that meeting, I was blessed with unexpected proximity to Maharishi. Shortly after I arrived in Seelisberg, a renovation began on Maharishi's apartment there and he temporarily moved his headquarters to the Hotel Hertenstein on the shore of Lake Lucerne. The hotel was a modern five-story building furnished in contemporary spare Swiss style. There, I was given a room directly beneath Maharishi's, and I discovered this location in a novel way. In early autumn, temperatures on the lake were somewhat warmer than in Seelisberg, although a lake fog cooled the air. It was not cold enough to turn on a heater, yet there was a source of heat filling my room that made it uncomfortably hot. I finally figured out that the heat was radiating down from the ceiling. Then I learned that the room I had been assigned was directly beneath Maharishi's. Around Maharishi there are no such things as coincidences. I was positive I was the beneficiary of the heat he was generating although I had no idea why and what it meant.

My first role on staff was as television cameraman, which meant standing behind a video camera on a tripod in front of Maharishi for hours at a time, often for an entire day, and sometimes until late into the night. Becoming a good cameraman meant learning to follow Maharishi's cues. I was unaware at first, but over time, I came to learn that Maharishi directed the sessions with very subtle gestures meant for the cameramen that remained unnoticed by everyone else. A quick flick of a flower in his hand, a subtle circle with a finger, a raised eyebrow, were all signals for the angles and perspectives the camera should be recording. Nobody taught me the cues; I learned them intuitively. Eventually, I came to believe that these instructions were done for our benefit—not only in our role as cameramen, but as devotees. On a deeper level they were meant to sync our mind to his. In the Hindu tradition, a devotee is expected to attune his mind to that of the master to attain his state of being. I was amazed to hear a longtime staff member say he knew the master's every desire—for a glass of water, a cup of tea—whatever it was—he knew. This attunement was most prevalent among Maharishi's cadre of secretaries, of which there were several at any given time.

My own reality was one of exhaustion. Especially when Maharishi remained on his couch all day conducting nonstop business. He had a superhuman ability to operate at an optimum level and go virtually without sleep. I found it impossible to keep up and sometimes sat back in a chair behind the camera and dozed off. I soon realized that however important others thought it was to record Maharishi's every word, I was not using my full potential standing behind a camera. I was a trained artist. In childhood, my parents recognized and nurtured my talent by hiring private tutors. I studied art in prep school and at Syracuse University College of Art. In Vietnam, a series of drawings of my infantry unit led to a job as Combat Correspondent. Maharishi must have heard my inner plea because, after a few weeks, he promoted me to the design staff.

My shift from cameraman to designer happened in a surprising way accompanied by a hilarious—mostly to Maharishi—scenario. One morning I walked into the meeting room where things were already underway, aiming for my usual position behind a camera. Maharishi caught my eye and pointed to an empty chair at the table set up for designers close to his dais. Lawrence Sheaff, the senior designer, sat at the far left. Next to him was Tony Miles, his English protégé. The empty seat was between Tony and another Brit, Anthony Ellis, also called Tony. Which meant there were three Tony's in a row. After I was seated Maharishi called on me, or so I thought. But, of course, as soon as he said "Tony," all three of us looked up together sending Maharishi into gales of laughter. The audience immediately got the joke and burst out laughing along with him, creating waves of joy. Just what I imagine Maharishi intended.

From then on, I was officially, and happily, known as one of Maharishi's designers.

Designers were at the top of Maharishi's hierarchy. When he was speaking, we sat at a table in the front row facing him.

Lawrence, who was at the apex and had Maharishi's total confidence, sat closest to him. If anyone had questions about an assigned project, Maharishi would often say, "Ask Lawrence." I was in awe of his talent, and learned a great deal from him. Being a designer meant synthesizing whatever Maharishi was expounding on—ranging from obscure knowledge from the Vedas, the ancient Hindu scriptures, to the practical systems of how to operate a local TM Center. All the while, we were gaining the experience of creating brochures, posters, and books, all useful real-world skills.

When Maharishi's apartment was finished and the headquarters moved back to Seelisberg, Eike Hartmannn, a designer I met at the course in La Antilla, invited me to share his office. Eike was in a special sphere all his own. He received his assignments from Maharishi privately and never sat with the other designers at the table. His office was barely large enough to accommodate two large drawing boards angled to lean against one another, but this arrangement turned out to be a wonderful gift for me. As we worked on our separate projects, Eike would patiently peer over the top of his board taking time to answer my questions about design projects or, generally, about the confusing world I had landed in. When we were in Spain, I had stuck my nose in his open doorway and asked him what it was like to work for Maharishi. I don't recall his answer, but just seeing him at work was enough to inspire me. It was then that the idea of becoming a devotee had begun to percolate. Now, in our shared space, Eike explained in his thoughtful, quiet way, how the mind of an enlightened master, being unbounded, might not always fit into what we might consider rational ways of acting. The master walked one step ahead of his disciples whose duty it was to try to keep up. Although a master's requests might seem unexpected and sometimes even impossible, he assured me that Maharishi had an exceptionally patient way of nurturing compared to some. I was already witnessing the unexpected side of Maharishi, plus the unfathomable side as well.

My initiation into the complete design/printing process occurred with a large ongoing project known as the "Festivals Materials." Maharishi felt it was important to celebrate the changing of the four seasons and he chose me to design and produce the materials, which included posters and brochures with his message. The materials were distributed globally with each season, including its opposite, for the opposing hemisphere. This meant designing winter and summer or spring and fall at the same time, giving each an appropriate look. In addition, all the pieces were translated into sixteen languages to include all the countries in which the Movement operated.

Everything the designers created was in support of the over-arching goal of the entire organization: To create a more peaceful world, one person at a time. The change of seasons was universal, something experienced by everyone on the planet, so the Festival Materials were an ideal opportunity to link Maharishi to a global audience. As the most recognizable image for the Movement, Maharishi's picture appeared on all printed materials and incorporating it in the design was important to ensure the success of any project. I looked at the festivals as my first big chance to show off my design skills.

I came up with what I was certain was a revolutionary new idea. I would keep the designs Maharishi preferred, traditional Roman typefaces, but I would take a radical turn from the Movement's staid English borders. I would replace them with a "living border," alive with the beautiful flowers Maharishi loved. Instead of printed gold lines framing Maharishi's picture, I envisioned a border of pink roses. I knew I was walking a fine line with my departure from the norm, but I was confident I could pull off a novel and beautiful set of materials. Luckily, my friend Victor Raymond, a photographer, signed onto my idea which involved photographing live roses set in straight lines that would become the borders. The idea was sound in theory but the reality was different. The delicate flowers wilted immediately under the hot studio lights. After several attempts of cutting the stems off, lining them up, and shooting them within seconds before they wilted, we were finally successful.

In the end, Victor was able to strip the films together in the montage department and combine the rose borders with Maharishi's photo in the center. This would be the image for the first-ever Spring Festival. Looking back, I see that because of the persistence of my ego, the designs went further over the edge than was necessary. If I had "asked Lawrence," as Maharishi instructed, if I had been willing to share my initial design with him, it may not have met with his approval, but a different design undoubtedly would have turned out just fine. But my ego had pushed me to keep my idea secret, knowing that if I shared it, it would have been altered and would no longer be "mine." I obviously had a long way to go before I was willing to let go of my ego and learn that the Festivals weren't about me leaving my mark as a designer, but about fulfilling Maharishi's wishes.

The Festivals weren't about Tony Anthony—but he didn't know that yet.

Each designer was entrusted with overseeing his project from beginning to end. Following weeks of design and prep work, the next phase was to oversee the printing process. With the films for my first project in the trunk of a car, I drove the finished films to the Movement's printing press in Rheinweiler, Germany, a village across the Swiss border from Basel, where I camped out for a week. Since this was my initiation into the world of printing, I became a student of the process. "Burning" metal printing plates from the films I had brought was the first step. The most difficult part was the printing process itself. As the designer I was entrusted with checking the press sheets for accuracy of color and sharpness as they came off the press. Admittedly, I was in over my head at first and "faked it 'til I made it." The German pressmen who were extremely exacting in their work, saw through me of course but were kind enough to guide me through the process.

When the posters were finally trimmed and the brochures were printed, folded, and bound, I was exhausted but elated with the results. I thought my "revolutionary" rose borders looked spectacular. I headed back to Seelisberg, fueled by my artistic achievement, to show the completed materials to Maharishi. I took the highway back through Basel to Lucerne and the mountain road up to Seelisberg buoyed by frequent stops for coffee. It was after midnight when I arrived with the Festivals' posters rolled up under my arm. Maharishi was deep into a talk when I entered the hall. I approached the edge of his dais as I had seen other designers do. Bursting with pride, I stood about ten feet from Maharishi's couch holding up a large poster for him to see. Moments passed without his acknowledging me. And then more time went by. And more, without Maharishi once glancing in my direction. When he ended his talk, I was positioned at the edge of the dais where he would step into his sandals. He had to walk right past me to exit the hall. When he finally stepped down from the dais, he stopped beside me. But rather than looking at the poster, he looked down. Then he stepped into his sandals and walked on as if I were invisible.

I was crestfallen.

I rolled up my poster and slunk back to my room searching for answers to why Maharishi ignored me. I wondered how I had screwed up. Or, perhaps he'd ignored me for a completely different reason. Had he changed his mind and felt the Festivals were no longer important? Whatever it was, I had no clue. No matter, I took it personally. I was hurt and upset and wanted to pack my grandfather's suitcase and leave Seelisberg. I closed the door to my room, lay down on my bed and fell asleep, my head spinning with thoughts, mostly about how I had failed to please the Master. Whatever the reason, my first big project was a failure.

After a night's sleep, I sat out on my balcony and did my usual meditation. Then I brought my roll of samples with me to breakfast as if I couldn't be without them until I discovered why they had displeased Maharishi so much that he wouldn't even look at them. After breakfast, I walked sullenly to my office and

I took my seat as usual at my drawing board across from Eike. I didn't have to say a word; Eike had witnessed what happened. He smiled at me over the top of his board with compassion and told me he had received the same lesson many times: *Non-attachment to outcomes.* Weeks later, when I had moved on to a new project and had all but forgotten the Festivals, Maharishi stopped me in the hallway to compliment me on the Festival materials. He knew, by then, that I had learned my lesson: I no longer cared about personal gain. I never heard a negative comment about the floral borders because I think the other designers were too kind to say anything. Over time, I concluded the posters were too sugary sweet, too much like Valentine's Day cards.

Finally, I was able to see through my own "big idea."

I vowed to change my strategy for the next Festivals, to find a photo of Maharishi that was so captivating on its own that the posters would not need some flashy design element. The slide collection of thousands of photographs of Maharishi was kept in a small storeroom just down the hall from our office. Some pictures were of him with dignitaries and saints who had visited Seelisberg, some were taken at various courses around the world. But the vast majority were of Maharishi seated on his deerskin on a white or gold silk-covered couch, surrounded by flowers in front of a painting of Guru Dev. The country didn't really matter, the setting in the photographs always looked pretty much identical. I realized though, that it was not the backdrop alone that was important, it was Maharishi's expression that mattered most.

Still searching, I went into the dark and stuffy room facing what I thought would be a week or more looking for a distinctive photograph. I vowed not to stop looking until I found the perfect picture, one that would truly inspire people. I had moved on from trying to satisfy my personal ego, to trying my best to do the right thing. Among the nearly limitless portraits of Maharishi, the variations of facial expressions were sometimes so subtle, that they were hardly noticeable. But the more I looked, the more I noticed subtle variations. At one point, I stopped to laugh. Something that Maharishi had said, floated to the surface: "Whatever we put our attention on grows stronger in our life." By putting my attention on the subtle distinctions, they began to reveal themselves. In fact, the variations of expressions I found in a single box of 24 slides were astounding. Even though they were taken just seconds apart, each one revealed an entirely new and different Maharishi.

The picture I had in mind, the one that would draw the viewer in, had to capture Maharishi in a moment of compassionate openness and joy. I pulled a few boxes of recent slides off a shelf, turned off the ceiling light, and flicked on a projector that was set up to face a screen. Someone had left a slide of Maharishi in the projector. *And there it was!* The shot I was looking for had already been selected. The image was not the usual head-on angle but a candid portrait of Maharishi out of doors holding a single red rose. The natural light was so much better than the harsh video lights that usually lit his stage. I recognized the shot as one Victor had taken a week earlier of Maharishi on the promenade overlooking the lake. I remembered thinking at the time, that that moment would make an exceptional photo. Victor had captured it. The look on Maharishi's face was one of pure bliss.

I made a full-color mockup using the photograph for the upcoming Summer Festival poster. When I showed it to Maharishi, he smiled his approval.

This said everything. The entire experience was a perfect example of how easily and beautifully life could function—when I took my ego out of the picture.

Welcome to Seelisberg

It took time before Seelisberg felt like home, and I have Eike Hartmann to thank for my sense of belonging. Eike, my cherished friend, together with his beautiful wife Renate, made me feel like part of their family. The Hartmann's open-heartedness imbued what often seemed like the otherworldly life of being on International Staff, as we were called, with a sense of real-world humanity. I understood why Maharishi had kept the Hartmanns so close for many years, and I was especially touched when they invited me to celebrate Christmas with them. Eike and Renate, and their newborn son, Gabriel, lived in an apartment above the dining room in the Waldhaus, a small inn the Movement rented to accommodate the expanding organization.

As I've said, my great good fortune was to share a tiny office with Eike. We were on the second floor of the Pilgerheim, the former staff quarters beside the Sonnenberg, where now most of the design and production of printed materials was done. The typesetter was one floor below us and the photo library was just down the hall. Editors and translators were stuffed into small, former bedrooms throughout the three-story building. During the day, and usually throughout the night, the lights in the Pilgerheim remained on. It was a bustling center of vibrant energy where everyone within was intent on accomplishing Maharishi's endless stream of projects. The devotion of Maharishi's staff, with his goals kept warm in their hearts, was unequaled to anything I have ever experienced, before or since.

I realized the honor that had been given to me as a member of the staff. Not only was I playing a part in fulfilling Maharishi's goal, I was learning the practical part of being a graphic designer. The art and design I studied in college were being made practical in the highest sense, with our goal of enlightening the world. My small role in achieving Maharishi's gigantic objective led me to the true value of devotion. Those who aligned their mind with the Master's were letting go of the personal and gaining the universal. I remember telling myself that the more I sunk my heart into being the Master's servant the less room there remained for me to suffer. This was really a selfish way to look at things, but when you get right down to it, spiritual seeking is a most selfish pursuit. The unexpected, yet very real result, went far beyond the ceasing of personal suffering, it brought about moments—and even entire days—of pure bliss. The joy of completing a project for Maharishi also came with believing there might be a karmic payoff not a monetary one.

Living in Seelisberg was reward enough in itself. It sometimes felt like Heaven on Earth. On the surface, Seelisberg was a typical Swiss mountain village of rolling green meadows below snow-capped mountains that was inhabited by more dairy cows than human beings. It was a picture postcard, imbued with serenity and a deep silence, the only exception being the blissful musical interlude of cowbells heard twice each day, once in the morning as the herds were led through town on the way to meadows and back again to the barn in the afternoon for milking.

Beneath the surface, on a much deeper level, was a very different village: Maharishi's cosmic version, a vision that was a model of what was possible on Earth. He was transforming a former summer resort for well-to-do Brits into The World Capital of the Age of Enlightenment.

Something unexpected snuck up on me personally. Somewhere along the way, I realized that a shift in consciousness had taken place without me noticing. This involved the dissolution of my ego. I had always believed I was running my universe, but I was finding that the universe was operating just fine without my instructions. I was much happier letting go of being in charge, and becoming part of the flow of life. My belief that I had been in control of my life turned out not to be the case at all. Finally, I saw that this was a lesson Maharishi had been teaching us all along. However, letting go of ego, while laser focused on trying to figure out and fulfill Maharishi's every thought, was difficult in the beginning. His slightest sign of displeasure was all it took to blast through anyone's ego. But eventually, I learned not to take such things personally.

Living so close to Maharishi, my individual hopes and dreams began to morph into his in a very real way. As I watched my consciousness expand, I recalled what Maharishi had told us in La Antilla, that being part of his World Plan was, by far, the most important job in the world. At the time, I thought he must be exaggerating, but now I discovered it was true.

The Celibate Life

The longer I was around Maharishi, the deeper into working on the individual he went. At one point, he announced that he expected celibacy of the members of International Staff. It was not a casual announcement—with Maharishi it never was—it was an absolute requirement. He told us that two years of total abstinence was enough to provide spiritual benefits for a lifetime. Even before meeting Maharishi, I had thought that celibacy would make for a simpler life. At one point I considered becoming a Catholic Jesuit. That would surely eliminate the drama a sexual relationship causes. Now I wondered whether letting go of sexuality, with all its accompanying downsides, would speed my spiritual evolution. But the decision was made simple because there was no choice.

Abstaining was easy because I was already there. I already felt a sense of greater personal power and well-being. I was in charge of my body rather than the other way around so in a way celibacy was a non-issue. Now that I was conscious of being celibate I saw that it was more about retaining energy and building a store of *Ojas*, a substance the body manufactures to give it greater strength.

For some unknown reason, by being celibate I felt less and less separation between myself and the cosmos. Eventually, as my body became accustomed to its higher role as a tool for evolution, the cosmos appeared to be contained more within me than without. Now I understood Maharishi's statement that the whole physiology is the expression of intelligence, of consciousness; that having a human body was the fastest way to evolve; that even angels— beings in non-physical form—sought the privilege of incarnating into a human body for that very reason.

One of the few quotes I've seen from Maharishi's beloved master Guru Dev was a powerful message on the subject.

"To get a human body is a rare thing—make full use of it. There are four million kinds of lives which a soul can gather. After that one gets a chance to be human, to get a human body. Therefore, one should not waste this chance. Every second in human life is very valuable. If you don't value this, then you will weep in the end.

"Because you're human, God has given you power to think and decide what is good and bad. Therefore, you can do the best possible kind of action. You should never consider yourself weak or a fallen creature.

"Whatever may have happened up to now may be because you didn't know, but now be careful. After getting a human body, if you don't reach God, then you have sold a diamond at the price of spinach."

Interestingly, on a trip to Lucerne, I got to experience the power of celibacy and the negative effect of its loss. At the newsstand near the quay, I was attracted to a picture of a pretty, blonde woman on a German magazine cover. Looking at the photograph created a powerful jolt of energy that felt like a lightning bolt running down my spine that caused an immediate excruciating pain in my lower back. Kundalini energy, life force or *prana*, flows *up* the spine with its force increasing as spiritual attainment increases. I had been enjoying the benefits of that energy flowing upward by experiencing wellbeing in all areas of my life. For me, even a single glance at a sexy magazine cover caused a painful reminder of the opposite effect, negative energy flowing *down* my spine.

Even with the power of celibacy, I was unapologetically drawn to women. No matter how many times I listened to someone extolling a life-long commitment to the celibate lifestyle, I felt two years would be enough. Of course, being a part of a group of celibate men was helpful. And Maharishi had organized our living arrangements to support the effort with the men cloistered up in the mountains in Seelisberg while the women lived in the valley in villages along the lake shore. Separation made celibacy easier for all.

The women, who were responsible for writing much of the Movement's literature, were an integral and equal part of Maharishi's World Plan. As far as I could tell Maharishi conferred with them daily and sometimes sent his car down to the lake to bring their leaders—Rindi Higgins, Sally Peden, Susan Watterson and Barbara Woods—to Seelisberg. I felt a personal sense of security when I passed them in the hall and felt no downward flow of Kundalini. It wasn't that they weren't attractive—they were.

Occasionally the male staff accompanied Maharishi down to the lake for a meeting with the women in a hotel dining hall. There were one or two women with whom I was smitten, but I was mindful of what Maharishi said—the more evolved we are, the narrower the path becomes.

Conversations on walks through the forest with friends like Eike, Victor and others often revolved around the role of a devotee. The first great monk of our tradition, Shankara, was often quoted. More than a thousand years before, he created the guidelines for the role of a Brahmachari, the Sanskrit term for a celibate monk. It was interesting to listen to married men praise the Brahmachari lifestyle. The goal was the same for all of us, to peel away attachments to everything in the way of living a life dedicated to the spiritual path, until there remained only devotion to the Master.

The definition used most often for the life of a devotee was the analogy of a river flowing into the ocean. The devotee is like the river moving towards the Master while the Master remains unmoving. The Master contains all knowledge necessary for the devotee to progress. The Master is everything. He is to be the supreme focus of the devotee until his or her entire being is given over. There is a tale about an acolyte who asked a learned elder if it was better to seek God directly or seek to find a guru first. The elder answered, "It is better to find a guru because it is the guru who shows you the way to God."

The Silence in My Room

I was permanently assigned a large room in Seelisberg on the top floor of the Kulm, three doors away from the entrance to Maharishi's apartment. Staff members tended to judge your status by the proximity of your room to Maharishi. Although only the room of Maharishi's top secretary was closer than mine, I never had the feeling that I was one of the "chosen ones." I felt that category belonged to people like Vesey Creighton, the master of ceremonies for the large meetings in the hall. And women like Rindi, Sally, Susan and Barbara who were given the seats in the assembly hall closest to Maharishi. And this elite group would also include the scientists like Geoffrey Clements with whom Maharishi could discuss the most current discoveries in the world of physics. There were others, of course, whose names were known by all and who were treated with deference befitting kings.

I was not on a level with this group, and even amongst Maharishi's designers I was not well known. Yet inwardly I knew Maharishi reserved a special place for me in his heart. Somehow, without trying, I was given special access to him, day or night. When I had a pressing question, he always greeted me warmly, gave me a deep sense of belonging and his full attention. I think there were only a few like his closest assistant, Brahmachary Nandkishore, who were aware of the bond between Maharishi and me.

As I became more comfortable with my role and my acceptance by Maharishi, my view of myself changed. I did not see myself as someone special, but just the opposite. When I thought of myself, which seemed to be less and less often, I noticed what had long been my pervading self-image, was fading away. I was slow to recognize this but, inevitably, the veil between the Relative and the Absolute was becoming thinner.

From my balcony, I could see a turret that protruded from the end of the building that belonged to Maharishi's bedroom. The curtains were always drawn, but I could usually sense his presence. Seeing his room gave me a profound sense of security. Images of war hardly ever intruded themselves into the deep silence pervading the Kulm, especially the Third Floor.

Opening the door to the hallway outside my room was like stepping into India. The air was almost always filled with the fragrant aroma of Indian spices. Maharishi's cook prepared meals in a room across the hall. Since Maharishi often entertained guests, the cook always made enough food for a dozen or more. Often, there was enough left over for hungry neighbors like me.

He made delicious perfumed rice, lentil dal, curried vegetables with Indian bread and gulab jamuns—doughnut balls dipped in sweet syrup—for dessert.

I felt tremendous gratitude for the privilege of living there.

And eating food prepared for Maharishi was an added grace.

The World is Not Real

The year I turned nine years old in this lifetime, my family moved into a stone mansion on a hill with a tennis court, meadows, and stables for horses. For our first Christmas Eve there, my parents followed the tradition of Santa secretly leaving our presents under the tree late at night while we slept. On Christmas morning, my sister Pati and I came down to the living room with great anticipation to see what Santa had left for us. I remember my parents being excited about the biggest present, which was mine that year, and they insisted that I open it first. Inside was a Lionel train set with tracks, a locomotive, passenger cars and a caboose, and a large black transformer with handles to operate the train.

Later that day my father and I installed the tracks in my bedroom using wooden blocks for buildings, creating a world in miniature. There were so many tracks that a section had to go under my bed, which really thrilled me because I imagined the train disappearing into a tunnel and coming out the other end. Who could've guessed that one day I would be living in Switzerland looking down at a scene with a train that disappeared into a tunnel and appeared at the other end? The Lionel brochure had pictures of sets built by hobbyists with a train like mine that traveled through villages, through tunnels, and over bridges. There were railroad stations with small figures of people waiting for the train to arrive. There were shoppers on the main street, trucks, cars, and police and fire stations, and everything a real town had, only in miniature.

Living in Seelisberg, I was constantly reminded of the miniature world of my train set. About a mile along the trail that led up the mountain behind the Sonnenberg, was a bench perched at the top of a cliff overlooking the lake, facing the town of Brunnen on the far shore. Seen from the cliff, Brunnen could've been one of the miniature villages in the Lionel brochure. Tiny people walked on a promenade beside the lake with cars and trucks moving along the road behind them. There were stores and houses and a church overlooked by mountains that could easily have been made of paper mâché. Toy-like steamers drew white lines on the surface of the lake and stopped at a dock to disembark miniature passengers. Some sunny days I sat on the bench munching on a chocolate bar totally engrossed in the scene.

It was easy to fall into this fantastical state of awareness in Seelisberg. Constantly being in Maharishi's darshan created moments that became hours and even days of joy. The world as

I once knew it began to appear completely unreal. No doubt the magical Swiss scenery helped create such a believable unreality. The real turned out to be unreal and the unreal real. It was far beyond being a daydream; the material world became transparent and, at times, would fade away until it disappeared completely.

I had read descriptions in the Vedas of the various "Lokas" or levels of existence beyond normal perception. This meant that the world we lived in was just one of many, which helped to instill it with an even greater sense of make-believe. I was almost certain that some divine being had created a world just for amusement, like a hobbyist would fashion mountains out of paper-mâché, stick plastic trees on the mountainsides, and sprinkle fake snow on the peaks.

My room on the top floor of the Kulm had an equally unearthly view. The balcony faced Mount Meru, as the huge monolith across the lake was now called, and had a spectacular view of the southern end of the lake. In the morning when the sun rose and the breeze came up and tickled the surface of the water, it glistened like liquid gold. At night the lights from houses and hotels along the shore twinkled like stars below, making it appear like I was floating in space.

When it snowed, a deep silence settled on Seelisberg and everything became muted and still. I felt as if I could touch the transcendent with my fingers; there was hardly a need to close my eyes. But when the sun shone after the clouds had passed, the snow glowed so brightly with celestial light that you couldn't bear to look, making the world disappear and me along with it.

Beneath Maharishi's Umbrella

I came to realize that Maharishi was a living expression of Pure Consciousness in its totality. It can be said that he *was* Pure Consciousness itself. Because he was in the flow of Consciousness beyond thought, what he might say could never be guessed, and to most of everyone he remained a great mystery. But what I began to experience, being close to him, was not *"This,"* the illusory relative world, but *"That,"* the unbounded, unchanging absolute field of pure Being.

Whenever I was in his presence, I witnessed my awareness expanding. At first, the sensation was overwhelming. My mind told me that my uncultured nervous system was not yet refined enough to adjust to this subtle more refined state. Although my expanded awareness was nowhere close to Maharishi's, there were times when a bolt of energy (kundalini) would flash up my spine as if my body was being repaired by some cosmic physician. The experience after was like floating in outer space without a tether. Finding itself in a field of unboundedness, the untethered mind would flail wildly trying to get a foothold on this new reality. But, it was obvious this was a place where the mind didn't belong.

All this having been said, I always felt at ease in Maharishi's presence. Even though the nervous mind might create anxiety when approaching him, when I came close, any discomfort suddenly disappeared. Even with a barrage of thoughts racing through my head, these, too, were washed away in his calm presence.

Always fascinating, each experience in Maharishi's presence was unique. Sometimes I felt as if all the molecules and cells in my body were dancing. At other times, I would feel like I was dissolving, that my body turned into nothing but cosmic energy. There could be lapses of time—missing spaces when it seemed nothing was said, nothing was seen or heard or thought. This timeless bliss was usual in meditation but not so much with the eyes open.

Maharishi was gracious and humble and, although his presence was kingly, he was equally accessible to everyone. One of the first things I had ever noticed about him was his perfect posture. He walked with the regal gate of a fearless warrior. Even though he embodied larger than life strength, he was very, very soft. His voice was so quiet that sometimes I couldn't make out his words yet, somewhat magically, whatever was said was understood. I often met with Maharishi to discuss a design project, either at its inception or when underway. His instructions were given in very few easily understood words, and I was never left with any doubt about the results he wanted.

One night, after his evening talk, I met with Maharishi when the hall was nearly empty and people had fallen into a kind of reverie as a result of his discourse. He wanted to speak to me about a project I was working on—I can't remember what it was. He beckoned me up onto the dais into a chair beside his couch. After I sat down, he gestured for me to come closer. I leaned towards him and he said, "Come closer. Come closer." I pulled the chair up until it was against the arm of the couch. He leaned over until he was inches from me and he remained that way, motionless. There was a look on his face as if he was working on something inside me. I have no idea what, but whatever it was, his darshan was so powerful, it felt transformative. After a few minutes, he said, "that's all," without discussing the project. But I knew that whatever needed to be taken care of and put right had been accomplished. In a daze, I put my palms together, heard the words "Jai Guru Dev" spoken by my heart, and walked off. Such encounters would, of course, seem unusual with someone other than Maharishi. But, with him, it seemed like business as usual— as if that's just what great sages do. I knew I had the good fortune to be in the presence of perhaps the greatest sage of our time.

It amazes me now to think that when I glimpsed Maharishi for the first time, as he stepped out of the convertible at Humboldt, I knew instantly that he was my guru, my lifelong teacher. Maharishi tells a story about his first meeting with his beloved teacher Guru Dev. It was at night and Guru Dev was sitting in the dark. A passing car flashed its headlights on his face for just a second. And in that instant, Maharishi knew. Just like I knew about him the first moment I laid eyes on him. We could attribute such recognition to many things—having been with him in a prior life, for one—but even that doesn't do the moment justice. For me, that first view of Maharishi was an instance of pure timelessness and grace. Although I didn't know it at the time, it was the grace of meeting the infinite embodied in human form. Can there be a more precious gift than that? Such moments, although they appear to last only for an instant, are timeless and eternal.

Anything is Possible

Maharishi was introducing a revolutionary idea: A global government that would govern on the level of Consciousness. The model was based on the belief that the daily practice of TM fosters peace and wellbeing in each individual. Therefore, if enough citizens of a country practice, the nation as a whole would benefit. Scientific studies had proven that positive benefits, some as dramatic as lowering the crime rate, were possible if only one percent of a population practiced Transcendental Meditation regularly. Thinking in global terms, Maharishi focused on countries whose leaders were receptive to his message of bringing fulfillment to all their people. And he believed that countries ruled by monarchs were the easiest to approach because only one person had to be convinced. Thailand seemed like a perfect place to start because of the royal family and a king who was beloved by his people. The king's birthday was approaching and Maharishi seized the occasion to make a personal presentation to him extolling the benefits of TM. Maharishi enshrined his message in a book, *The World Government for the Age of Enlightenment.*

The text of the book had already been typeset and Maharishi wrote a personal message for members of Thailand's parliament and one especially for the king. I was given the job of designing a cover for the parliamentary edition as well as a royal edition of one. The king's version was to have a padded maroon velvet cover with his name stamped in gold. Timing was critical. The books had to arrive in time for the king's birthday celebration, just a few days away. Maharishi's final instructions to me were, "Make certain you *personally* see the books being loaded on the plane." His words made an indelible imprint on my mind. How, I thought, was it going to be possible for me, personally, to view cartons of books loaded onto a cargo plane? I was confident in my ability to manage every step up to that, but, frankly, had no idea how that might happen. My mind told me that people are not allowed in secure cargo areas, especially not at a huge airport like Frankfurt where the books were to be shipped from.

But that was somewhere in the far-off future. First came the printing and production. I knew the press in Rheinweiler already had a long list of projects, all undoubtedly given top priority by Maharishi. Mine was just one more to add to the list. Arriving in Rheinweiler with the films for the book in hand, I naively assumed my project would go to the head of the line. I met with the director of the press, a capable German named Eberhardt, who was used to designers arriving from Seelisberg insisting Maharishi had given their project top priority. I followed Eberhardt into his office where he pointed to a chalkboard on the wall with about a dozen jobs ahead of mine. He wrote "Thailand Book" on the bottom, and faced me with a smile. Evidently, I didn't rank very high in Eberhardt's estimation. I wasn't just a designer from Seelisberg, I was *the newest designer.* Add to that: I wasn't German, or even English—I was *American.* I had been warned early on that Americans weren't highly regarded in Rheinweiler.

Nonetheless, I didn't feel that Eberhardt held any animosity towards me, and I could see why Maharishi had put him in charge. He was at once friendly yet immovable. Luckily, having been a sergeant in the infantry had taught me something about getting things done. The situation needed a dramatic move. I asked to use his phone and dialed the number Nandkishore had given me to reach Maharishi in Seelisberg. Nandkishore picked up immediately and I outlined the situation explaining that given the list of projects before mine, the timeframe for what Maharishi asked me to do wouldn't be possible. Nandkishore, in his soft imperturbable way, asked to speak to Eberhardt. I handed the phone to Eberhardt who listened intently with a stoic expression on his face revealing nothing, until I heard, faintly, Maharishi speaking to Nandkishore. I watched Eberhardt's expression soften. When he hung up, he turned to the scheduling board and wrote "King of Thailand" across the top. Like any good soldier, he knew to obey an order from the commander. The project suddenly had top-priority and now there was a chance that the King of Thailand might receive his birthday present.

Part One of the miracle.

The pre-press work—plate-making and printing—began immediately and continued through the night. After coming off the press, the ink needed time to dry before the books could be bound. But by the next afternoon, a thousand bound books were stacked on wooden pallets, waiting. I was most concerned about the king's copy, but I had total confidence in the Germans, who were meticulous about their work. As expected, the final product, bound with its padded velvet cover and the king's name stamped in glittering gold, was perfect. It looked and felt royal. We wrapped the king's copy in its own box with plenty of protective padding and secured it on top of the pallet.

With the pallet loaded into the back of a press van, and with instructions to the Frankfurt Airport in hand, I took the wheel and headed onto the autobahn. I was exhausted and I knew my journey wouldn't be finished until I had seen the books loaded on the plane. Eberhardt had arranged to have the pallet shipped aboard a Thai Airlines flight from Frankfurt to Bangkok, which departed five hours hence—the amount of time I was told it would take to drive to Frankfurt.

Exactly five hours later I pulled into Germany's largest airport, reading signs written in German, trying to guess what the word "freight" or "cargo" might be. I followed trucks instead of cars and was led to the gated entrance to a group of huge hangars. When I showed the shipping document to the man in the guardhouse, he pointed to a hangar and told me to hurry. The plane was loaded and about to depart. I could hardly believe how easy it had been to gain access to the hangar. Through the open doors of the hangar I could see a giant Thai Airlines 747 cargo plane just as its cargo bay was closing. Beeping the horn on the van, I raced up to the plane. As I came to a stop, a man approached and read the shipping document I handed him. He spoke into his walkie-talkie and I watched the cargo door stop and re-open. A forklift appeared and plucked the palette of books out of the back of the van, sped toward the plane, lifting the pallet into the open cargo bay as I watched in amazement.

Part Two of the miracle: I saw it happen.

Once the cargo bay was closed and the books were locked inside, my exhaustion became elation. I felt as if I had hardly done a thing. But somehow, it had all happened flawlessly. I'd merely been the witness.

"Maharishi Wants to See You."

$\mathcal{I}$was asleep one night when Brahmachari Nandkishore knocked on my door and woke me. Looking into the depth of his dark brown eyes, I barely heard him say in his soft voice, "Maharishi wants to see you." As he walked out, I dressed quickly and met him again holding the door open to Maharishi's apartment. He led me into the sitting room where Maharishi was reclining on a divan with his arm over a bolster and his hand supporting his head. Until then, I had never seen Maharishi lying down, only sitting cross-legged on a couch or walking. I'd once read that it was a privilege to be allowed to see the Master in repose.

Maharishi motioned me to sit on the floor beside him, and even this casual acknowledgment made me feel as welcomed as a family member invited to join a private conversation.

Vernon Katz, a soft-spoken English scholar and one of

Maharishi's dearest friends, was settled into a comfortable chair at the base of the divan, reading from a letter. I caught on quickly that the letter was from Max Fleischer, initially the course leader for my teacher training, who had inexplicably disappeared in the middle of the course. I gathered that the letter had been addressed to Vernon, but meant for Maharishi's ears. In it, Max extolled his new life in the English countryside. Vernon paused and held up a photograph accompanying the letter for Maharishi to see. Max and a young woman, whom I recognized as his assistant on the course, posed beneath a rose trellis in front of a small English cottage.

Maharishi sighed. "Just imagine," he said, "Max left me for a cottage in England. I gave him the unbounded universe, yet he chose a cottage with flowers."

Maharishi sat up and turned, looking down directly into my eyes while holding his hand, palm down, in the air. "When you are with me, I take you from here," he said, raising his hand a few inches, "to here… to here." Each time, he raised his hand a few inches higher. "If you leave when you are here—" he held out his hand, "that is where you stay. You never make it to the next level." Then he added, as a kind of afterthought, "not until you come back." There was little doubt why Maharishi was telling me this. As he spoke, I sensed that at some point my leaving was inevitable.

I was aware of a huge contradiction in me. As I took in Maharishi's words, I felt my mind expanding and filling with love, something that always happened in his presence. And yet, there was a basic disagreement with what he was saying. I had always prided myself on being a self-sufficient individual. From a very early age, my father instilled self-sufficiency in me. He convinced me that it was an essential survival skill—one that had worked for him. It worked for me as well. Believing in my resourcefulness helped me survive a war.

But as I listened to Maharishi, I heard him telling me he was responsible for my evolution. Given my recent experience, I had no doubt this was true. I had been evolving at light-speed ever since Maharishi had found me, but at the same time I knew in the end, that it would be impossible for me to entirely let go of creating my own destiny.

I'd once heard that enlightened masters sometimes teach their students by somewhat nefariously telling them the opposite of what they needed to hear. Much later, when I considered what Maharishi had told me, I thought that really what he was teaching me was to find the truth within myself.

At the time, however, I felt that I might be an ignorant fool for believing I knew better than my enlightened Master—and, I was convinced by then, that Maharishi was indeed enlightened— but, what I also considered that within Maharishi's darshan, I was unbound by space or time. In this case I was seeing into the future and recognizing my karmic inevitability. At some point, I would need to make my way in the world of space and time without being under the protection of Maharishi's umbrella.

But at that moment, I had a reprieve from making a choice because what would take place would happen in the future. When it did occur, it would not be a conscious decision as much as an inevitability. I watched my mind trying to grapple with this on its own level, but being in Maharishi's presence, I was enfolded in Pure Consciousness itself, far beyond what the mind could comprehend.

I would have to wait and let time tell.

This meeting with Maharishi has remained with me more than any other. I was keenly aware of my expanded consciousness, the witness watching the humorous ruminations of Tony's mind at work. Maharishi's darshan was palpable as he leaned over the edge of his bolster, peering down at me. His words had been like a pin-prick on my body that had expanded to infinite proportion. I was aware of not being limited to just a singular point of view, or even Maharishi's point of view. My awareness included infinite angles or perspectives, which made me realize I had access to unlimited ways of looking at what he was telling me. If I cared to parse them all, I knew it would be impossible for the mind to try and catch up so I didn't try.

It was an amazing revelation to know there are no limits to the number of variations we can experience. This realization made me aware of how much we humans constrain our thinking. I knew, then, that I could see as deeply as I wanted into whatever subject I chose—and even into all subjects at once if I so desired.

What was obvious is that we really are unbounded Pure Consciousness itself. And, since there is no such thing as *time* in what is an infinite state of being, I wouldn't have to wait to find out. The answers to everything—for all time—were there right in front of me, for me to know now. I saw that the decision I would make—seemingly in the future—was already a done deal.

Soaring

"Someday," Maharishi said dreamily as he stared out the window during a meeting in the hall in the Sonnenberg, "we will all be flying around Mount Meru across the lake.

The *flying* he meant was flying without mechanical means.

I had always loved flying, especially in helicopters. As a combat correspondent in Vietnam, I flew in helicopters almost every day. Heading to where the action was, I would ride out to the field from my base usually sitting atop crates of C-rations and ammunition. Then I would hitch a ride back on another chopper sometime later when I had my story and photographs.

The Movement owned a small Hughes helicopter to ferry Maharishi from Seelisberg to the advanced meditation courses in various parts of Switzerland. Maharishi's pilot, Greg, had been a helicopter pilot in Vietnam during the same years I was there.

Although we never met in-country the war connects all veterans and so we became friends. He would invite me to ride along on refueling runs to Zurich because it was better for flying to have some added weight in the fluky winds of the Swiss mountains. Greg was, by the way, the only non-Swiss pilot certified to fly helicopters in the country because of the inherent danger of Alpine weather.

The helipad was just up the road from the capital, and taking off from there was always a thrill. Only moments after we lifted off and gained enough altitude to dip the nose and gain forward momentum, the ground plunged away and we went from being just fifty-feet from the ground to over a thousand-feet above Lake Lucerne. It felt like the Earth had suddenly dropped away. With the sudden change in temperature, caused by the cool air from the lake, the tiny helicopter dropped dramatically before finally leveling out. It was always a thrill to fly in the tiny aluminum and Plexiglas bubble.

On one refueling trip, I shared the front passenger seat with Walter Koch, who as an ex-aeronautical engineer, was genuinely interested in the flight capabilities of helicopters. He challenged Greg with questions while I listened in on my headset. Walter explained that according to some aeronautical theories, a helicopter should not be able to fly. Quite interesting to hear as we zoomed across the lake to Zurich. I shared a piece of trivia of my own. Igor Sikorsky, the inventor of the helicopter, built his first prototype in my great-grandfather's barn on Long Island. My mother's stories of listening to the roar of his engines as a child inspired my fascination with helicopters and flying in general.

Greg had great stories about flying with Maharishi. He told me that once when he was flying Maharishi to a course in France, in the highest part of the Alps near Mont Blanc, they arrived when the hotel below was completely fogged in. Greg prudently thought they should not attempt a landing, but Maharishi assured him he could guide them safely down through the heavy fog. Because they would be attempting a landing in a ski resort without being able to see ski lift towers and cables, Greg was wary. But, then again, it was Maharishi assuring him that everything would be alright. Greg began the descent being guided solely by Maharishi's hands held up in front of him, angling them to one side or the other, instructions to move to the left or right. Within minutes, following Maharishi's hand motions, the helicopter emerged from the fog exactly dead-center on the helipad beside the hotel.

Years later, I was given another quite spectacular chance to fly during an advanced meditation course at Amherst College in Western Massachusetts. This time it was in a brand-new twin engine turbo-prop plane, one of two the Movement had leased. I was invited to join on a mission to pick up printed materials in New Jersey. The load of paper was heavy enough to require both planes, and afforded an opportunity for the pilots to show off their amazing skill. Flying in tandem, we headed south from North Hampton Airport beneath a powder blue sky accented by puffy white clouds—a perfect day for flying. There was a stunning view below of the Berkshire Mountains in Massachusetts, and the rolling hills of Connecticut. Nearing the New York metropolitan area, we descended and followed the Hudson River to Teterboro Airport just across from Manhattan.

Flying back to Massachusetts both planes soared above the puffy white clouds side by side. I heard the two men at the controls, both ex-Airforce fighter pilots, chatting over the radio about having some fun. Before I could even think what that meant, the other plane flipped onto its side and dove nearly straight down toward the earth. Seconds later we followed, flipping on *our* side plunging close to the other plane's tail, playing follow the leader. Now I was onto the game. We were the attack aircraft in pursuit of an enemy fighter. We kept up the chase, circling around and under a cloud, then climbing back up to where we'd been. As my head returned to nearly normal, my pilot glanced over with a smile. I heard in my headset, "Doing okay?"

I wasn't quite sure but no matter, because no sooner had he asked than the other plane flipped sideways again, so did we, and down we went a second time. Again, a chase, zooming through the space between clouds, circling around them, and heading up again. It was exhilarating! The acrobatics seemed totally automatic for the two pilots. No thinking involved, completely effortless.

When we returned to altitude above the clouds for the second time, the show wasn't over. There was more. Flying side-by-side in smooth air, the two planes inched closer and closer together until we were so close, we could see the other pilot's teeth when he smiled. Our plane slowly inched down and then slid *under* the other plane just feet beneath its belly. It was insanity for two planes flying at 200 miles an hour to be maneuvering so close, yet the performance was so skillful it felt natural. Then we slid out from underneath and inched back up until the two planes were again side-by-side. Next came the grand finale. The planes inched closer and closer again until the other plane's wing was just a sliver above ours. With the wingtips overlapping, the other pilot tapped our wing. The movement, so adept and precise, took my breath away. With a nod and a smile, the two pilots smiled at one another, before the other plane dove down, one last time, before landing back at North Hampton Airport.

The Space Above the Lake

Nearly every morning, I sat out on my balcony not only to meditate but to take in the extraordinary view. There were the mountains and the lake resting below, a huge silent but lively presence. Some days, especially in the early morning or late afternoon, the waves glistened bright gold. Moreover, the view created an enclosed space that intrigued me more and more as time passed. I had no idea why, but the empty space began to overpower even the intense beauty of the surroundings. It became a holy space imbued with unspoken meaning. Trying to find what was contained there, I studied the emptiness by squinting or shifting my eyes from side to side, attempting to change the way it was perceived. The only immediate result was, with a certain focus, I could see tiny sparkles of light that swirled around crazily. They were similar to the pinpricks of light I saw with my eyes shut tight.

The result was not spectacular. That is, until one day when I happened to be particularly distracted by something—a project I was working on, or my annoyance with a staff member, I don't remember what it was—but I noticed the space in front of me had changed all on its own. It had inexplicably gained substance, which made me realize why the space intrigued me so. The empty space was just as much an object as the mountains were—or the lake or the clouds in the sky.

So, the reason why I found it so captivating made perfect sense. The empty space wasn't empty at all. Before, it never made sense to be intrigued by emptiness, but now that it was known as a *thing* or a *something,* emptiness had a value and had become quite interesting.

I thought: What if empty space wasn't just another *thing,* but the container of all things? What if this *emptiness* was the *fullness* Maharishi talked about? What if it was the *That* with a capital T— the *That* in "all This is That?"

Whatever it was, the mind reached its breaking point—the edge beyond which it could not go. Could it be, I wondered if I was getting closer to Reality with a capital "R" only I didn't know it. If the mind couldn't know it, then what could? How could I be sure?

The answer was, I couldn't. All I knew is that my mind had been out-smarted, out-distanced, out-everythinged.

So, eventually the mind itself saw that it was what needed to be let go. It was useful to a point but it sensed that enlightenment couldn't happen if it was in the way. Enlightenment was not an intellectual thing, it was a consciousness thing. If I was to truly become the white cinema screen on which creation was projected,

"I" was what needed to get out of the picture.

I, or the person I thought of as "Tony," had to remain left behind. The thought that Tony would become cosmic was merely a thought. But when Maharishi explained "all This is That," he wasn't speaking on the thinking level. It might even be said that, in reality, it wasn't even Maharishi doing the speaking; it was the totality of Pure Consciousness speaking. And, it wasn't speaking to the individual known as Tony, it was actually speaking to the Pure Consciousness in him.

This made perfect sense, even to the mind. It made sense that often, after speaking with Maharishi, there was much I couldn't remember that appeared as blank spots in the conversation. Evidently, the witness—or Pure Consciousness—would be awake in me at times and sometimes not.

My conclusion was that enlightenment doesn't actually happen to an individual; it happens to itself. Maharishi has said, "When we say total reality of consciousness, we mean consciousness in its self-referral state, where consciousness knows itself and nothing else. This state of consciousness is Pure Consciousness."

So, Tony wasn't what was to become enlightened—that was never going to happen. And the "witness" that was often talked about, wasn't Tony either. The witness was nothing but Pure Consciousness looking through Tony's eyes. Enlightenment meant Pure Consciousness was using Tony's nervous system as a vehicle. Tony was just a vehicle for Pure Consciousness to find completion, to be the fullness of Itself in a human body on Planet Earth.

Everything in existence, is nothing but Pure Consciousness. Humans, having a human mind, are blessed—or *cursed*, depending on how you look at it—with free will. This is how the Creator experiences Pure Consciousness fully, by allowing humans the freedom of participating or not. This is the *Lila*, the play of life.

Ivan

*I*n Seelisberg, the expansion of consciousness was always at the forefront, so there was hardly time for paying attention to the social aspects of life, but I was lucky to have a few meaningful friendships. Ivan Stuffle was one.

Ivan was an accomplished sculptor in Sweden in the prime of his career when he accepted Maharishi's invitation to come to Seelisberg to sculpt a life-size statue of Maharishi's beloved master, Guru Dev. To understand his trust in Ivan, one should know that Maharishi's love for his beloved teacher was the entire focus of his life. Everything he did, he did for Guru Dev.

As soon as I heard that Ivan had arrived, I set out to meet him. After all, I had been a lifelong student of art. When I approached him in the dining room to introduce myself, he drew back with a look of shock on his face. Just to acknowledge my presence, he seemed to emerge out of a deep silence. As I got to know him I realized he was the most inward and solitary man I'd ever met. He had the heart and soul of an artist. He was small, wiry and strong, but with a gentle demeanor and he spoke so softly, it was difficult to hear him. In a way, he seemed almost invisible. I explained that I was eager to meet him because of my love of art, and when I told him that I was one of Maharishi's designers, he seemed to warm up a bit. I suggested that, perhaps, when he had some time, we could talk about art. Although he seemed amenable to the idea, I didn't see him for weeks after our encounter. He told me later that he had been busy around the clock working on an armature for his sculpture and he spoke about it with such intensity that I suspected his absence at meals meant he had simply forgotten to eat.

Maharishi arranged for Ivan to have a high-ceilinged, light-filled studio overlooking the lake. It was announced that the studio was strictly off limits to everyone including Maharishi's closest staff. Even after we became good friends, I understood his need to work in private and never asked to see his work. He told me that Maharishi requested that no one did.

He surprised me one day by sitting down across from me in the dining room. He remembered my interest in art, he said, and we had our first of many discussions on the subject. To begin, he asked me who my favorite artists were. I brought up the Renaissance artists—Da Vinci and Botticelli. He admired them as well, he said, but when he mentioned several of his favorite painters, I was embarrassed to admit that I had never heard of them. This was the beginning of my education into many superb but overlooked painters and sculptors. When Ivan joined me at the table again the next day, he reached into the well-worn leather pouch he always carried, and pulled out a stack of postcards, reprints of paintings of the artists we had discussed the previous day. Each card came with fascinating insights into the work. My mind flashed back to my art history professor's slide shows with her sleep-inducing, lifeless commentary. But as Ivan revealed the subtleties of exquisite works of art, I was amazed and moved. When he realized that my interest was genuine, he joined me for meals often.

We shared another common bond; a need to escape the constricted life in Seelisberg. We both loved coffee which was nowhere to be found in town. So Ivan drove us, like two escaped convicts, in his tiny Citroën truck—the kind used all over France and Switzerland as delivery vans—down the mountain road to the highway and into Lucerne. We made the trip frequently enough to acquire a favorite café and even a preferred table, where we energized ourselves with delicious Swiss pastries washed down by lattes and cappuccinos. We sat at the very edge of the quay overlooking the Kapellbrücke, the ancient wooden covered bridge, which Lucerne is famous for. It was wonderfully relaxing to escape into the simple world of people watching. In Medieval times, the bridge was used as a place of torture. Now, it was a major tourist attraction. It crossed the spillway from the lake linking the old town to the new.

When we weren't talking about art, our conversations touched on the steady stream of tourists from all over the world. I enjoyed the Americans the most, who stood out as the loudest and most noticeable. I remember one of my countrymen, in a screaming yellow shirt and cowboy hat, yelling to his wife heading across the bridge, "Wait, Honeybun, I found another chocolate shop!"

We didn't spend all our time studying the odd behavior of humankind. On one trip we took in a breathtaking show at the Lucerne Museum of Art. The artist had hung large—twenty-feet or more—canvases from the ceiling like banners. The paintings consisted of simple horizontal lines of brilliant, saturated colors. Their vibrant, worldly hues evoked a lively set of emotions. In striking contrast, the more understated, pastel colors we used in Maharishi's designs were meant to settle the mind into a subtler, more peaceful place. This brought to mind how the world contains everything from the gross to the subtle and everything in between.

As much as I felt incredibly blessed to be a part of the monkish world of Maharishi's ashram, it didn't end my love affair with the world of bright colors and sharp edges. The paradox was that being with Maharishi had increased my appreciation of *all* my surroundings. I could see the bold and finer attributes of the material world more clearly and feel its powerful attraction. The more sensitive my awareness became, the more beautiful *everything* appeared. As I left my personal attitudes behind—my New England bred prep school snobbishness, I could see the beauty in everyone, even tourists, and something as simple as the colors of their clothes. After all, weren't they the same colors the artist used in his paintings in the Lucerne Kunstmuseum? Weren't the tourists themselves wearing a breathtaking display of reds and yellows, blues and greens?

The contrast of life in Lucerne helped me to see my life in Maharishi's ashram more perceptively. Although I loved being close to Maharishi, existence in such a structured and isolated society was sometimes hard to take. As in any such place, there was jealousy of those who attained power because they had been around Maharishi longest, and envy of those who were rumored to have achieved higher states of consciousness. Generally speaking, no one but Maharishi himself—and the saints that visited from time to time—had awakened to a higher state.

Viewing Seelisberg from the clarity of a café table in Lucerne, I recognized the patronizing attitude that those of us in the Movement carried in our suit pockets. Those who considered themselves to be among the spiritually fittest referred to the world beneath us as "the great swamp of the ignorant." I had to be vigilant, to watch that I didn't fall prey to that that sort of condescending behavior. Although I was well aware that I was privileged to live under the tutelage of an enlightened Master, I knew that, more than anything, I was just plain lucky. Call it "good karma."

At times, it became obvious that being on the path to enlightenment meant witnessing the unfolding of past Karma. On one trip to Lucerne, when Ivan and I were walking across the Schwanenplatz heading to our café, we passed a newsstand that sold the *International Herald Tribune*, with stories from the *New York Times* and *Washington Post*. I bought a copy and was astounded by a front-page article about Kate Webb, an Australian UPI reporter I had met and fallen in love with in Vietnam. This confluence of events, to be walking by the newsstand on that particular day, when that particular story appeared, was incredible. The story was about four Western journalists who had been ambushed in a jeep by Communists from Cambodia and believed to be dead. The body of a white female had been among the four and was presumed to be that of Kate Webb.

I had long ago buried my feelings for Kate along with the rest of the Vietnam War. Because it was something I never talked about, Ivan was surprised to hear I had been a soldier in the war. I never brought it up because it seemed antithetical to Maharishi's teaching to bring up such a negative topic. My reticence to speak about Vietnam didn't mean I regretted my past. On the contrary, I felt that having experienced the most horrific aspect of the real world gave me an advantage. Even so, I felt it was better to keep my experience of the war private. During my last months in Vietnam, while I was still deeply in love with Kate, she had been transferred to the UPI Bureau in Phnom Penh Cambodia. Before departing, she wrote to me that she was sad to be leaving me, and she sent me some beautiful temple rubbings from the ancient Hindu temple Angkor Wat in Cambodia. Thoughts of her leaving Vietnam made me love her even more and I wrote to tell her that I wanted us to be together after I had completed my tour. I received a devastating response when she admitted, for the first time, to being in a long-term relationship with her bureau chief. Even though learning about Kate's death was a shock, reading the story helped me to let go of the relationship.

It was a relief to be able to finally share my story with Ivan, a man with the sensibility to understand. He revealed his own struggle with unrequited love, which helped me put mine in perspective. Ivan was at least ten years older, and had experienced the world as well, which is why I felt I could impart my feelings to him. I was not the only man in Seelisberg with a prior life of some consequence. This unspoken understanding between us showed me that even in the fairy-tale world of Seelisberg, it was possible to be real and to reveal actual emotions.

Driving uphill back to our ascetic life in the mountains, we were birds flying up to a nest somewhere high above the clouds.

A New Suit

No matter how long I was in Seelisberg, soaking up the meditative atmosphere and the lifestyle, I always kept one foot in the Relative World, and so I took another occasional opportunity to come down from the mountain by volunteering to make the trip to the art store in Zurich to pick up supplies for the designers. The journey began with a short steamer ride across the lake to Brunnen, timed to meet the train to Zurich. Arriving at Hauptbahnhof, one of the busiest train stations in the world, was a sudden immersion into the sights and sounds of a bustling Swiss city. There were shops of all kinds and food vendors with their tantalizing smells—perhaps, especially for a vegetarian— of the sausages with mustard the Swiss loved. Crowds always surrounded the stand-up counters at the entrance to the huge station. I stifled my impulse to buy one by thinking, "sin of all sins," and walked on straight through the enormous station and onto the street.

The trek from there crossed a narrow stone bridge, the demarcation of Zurich's old town which was endlessly fascinating to me. The art store was in the heart of the artsy, offbeat section, home to Zurich's outstanding Kunsthaus Art Museum and filled with galleries. There were stores of every sort selling glittery, well-lit items displayed to be coveted. Walking the cobblestone streets was the polar opposite of strolling the forest trails of Seelisberg. Like my trips to Lucerne with Ivan, Zurich was an injection of the material world into the bloodstream, a shot I desperately needed to maintain equanimity. It was like a tranquilizer that calmed the righteous but, for me, the uptight sensibility of the brahmacharya lifestyle. I often wondered how others could be at peace with themselves with the restrictions of being celibate, vegetarian, and ostensibly thinking only pure thoughts twenty-four hours a day.

The art store, to me, was a heaven of creative possibilities. I enjoyed the feel and touch of the paper in the drawing pads, the smell of the colored pencils, and the bright colors of the felt-tipped pens. Over time, I came to know the German names for colors: Rot, Grun, Blau, Gelb, Weiss und Schwartz. Then, there was always a chance to visit the Kunsthaus which had an inspiring collection of the Swiss artist Paul Klee, whose small works incorporated vibrant colors into precise graphic shapes. His amazing paintings gave me the nourishment I needed.

One afternoon, arriving back at the station with time to spare before my train back to Brunnen, I took a stroll down Zurich's Bahnhofstrasse known as "the most expensive street in the world."

The top Italian designers, Armani, Gucci, and others, had shops with elegant window displays of men's and women's clothing, shoes, and accessories. My love of design of every kind included fashion, especially the menswear I could imagine for myself. I stared at the elegant clothing, astounded by the exceptional high quality. There was nothing comparable in America. I found myself coveting suits I could not possibly afford.

Or so I thought.

I never wanted to stand out. I preferred, more than anything, to remain anonymous. But there were incremental changes taking place all along, made not by me but by Mother Nature. One of these was in the way I dressed. I stopped in front of a window with a mannequin wearing a beautiful tan suit. The color was perfect, so subtle it was like sand on a beach. I wasn't sure, but the fabric seemed to be linen or a combination of linen and something softer, perhaps silk or cotton. The point is, the suit captured me.

While I stood frozen in place, enthralled and imagining how I would look in the suit, the shop door opened and out stepped an older gentleman. I guessed he was Italian, and he had a winning salesman's smile. He seemed nothing like the stylish young salespeople in the other shops whom I found rude and unapproachable. Here was a friendly gentleman who spoke broken English with an Italian accent. I liked him immediately, but I was afraid he had mistaken me for a rich American tourist who could afford the suit, which probably cost as much as a car.

I was about to explain that I was "just looking" when he suggested I try it on. Not wanting to lead him on, I said I was certain the suit was well above my price range.

"Why worry about the price?" he said, holding the door open for me. Before I knew it, the elegant fragrance of fine fabrics and luxurious leather drew me into the store. I was offered a seat in a velvet chair as soft as a cloud while the man hurried to the window for the tan suit jacket. I stood and, in no time, he slid the silk-lined jacket over my arms and shoulders and buttoned two buttons on the front. He tugged it down sharply and smiled. It fit like it had been tailored for me and felt better than I imagined a suit jacket could feel. The cut was Italian—tight around the chest with proud squared-off shoulders, nothing like the baggy American jacket I walked in with. I could barely feel the light and silky touch of the material. The blue suit I owned was a used Chevrolet compared with this expensive Mercedes.

I had grown up in a family where clothes were important. My father had been born a poor kid in Boston, so when he moved to New York his image was extremely important to him. When he went off to work in the morning, he was always, as my mother said, "dressed to the nines." Al Anthony, the Madison Avenue advertising maven, attributed much of his success to how he presented himself. When I was a young man, he impressed upon me the importance of projecting success. "People judge you by what you wear" was his belief. When he met my mother, eight years his junior, he created a career for her as a fashion model, and always saw that she was dressed in the latest fashions. She loved expensive clothes and never went to the grocery store without wearing a beautiful dress and a string of pearls or a gold bracelet.

Because I attended private schools from an early age, I was used to dressing in a coat and tie. In prep school, the dress code was a school blazer with button-down shirt and a regimental striped tie over grey flannel slacks and cordovan leather loafers. Later in the army, stateside, we wore uniforms starched and pressed above spit-shined boots. What mattered most to me now was the design, the quality of the fabric and how well a garment was constructed. This had nothing to do with snobbery and everything to do with being conscious of a finer level of quality.

The Italian salesman knew I was in love with the suit. And although I continued to insist that the price was beyond my means, that didn't appear to be an obstacle to him. For whatever reason—I have no idea what—he told me not to worry, he would find a way to make the suit mine. The key turned out to be my profession. When he asked me, I told him I was a meditation teacher. The word teacher just rolled off my tongue. For a reason I didn't understand, he was excited immediately. Exclaiming, "Professore! Professore!" in Italian, he rushed off through a door at the back of the store. Minutes later, he appeared, smiling, and said the owner had taken pity on the meager salary teachers earned and insisted on selling the suit to the "professore" at whatever price was affordable.

We worked out a price I was comfortable with that was considerably less than what the suit was worth. Before I could believe what was happening a tailor appeared from the back of the shop with a yellow tape and a pin cushion. He measured me carefully from head to toe, fitting the shoulders and sleeves on the jacket, the waist, the length and the inseam of the trousers. I may have been raised in an upper-middle class family, but that was long past. Now I was working for free, believing I was helping the world, and had only a few hundred dollars left in savings. I wrote a check for most of that savings and thanked the salesman for making the sale happen.

I walked out in a state of amazement. The fulfillment of my desire to own a beautiful suit was nothing short of miraculous. In Maharishi's teachings, this fulfillment is known as "Nature's support," a manifestation in the Relative world of our desires. On the train ride back to Seelisberg, I conjured up theories about how I had gained this largesse, but concluded I didn't need to know. It made me happy to think I was being provided for, and that I must be doing something right.

Bridging the Gap

Maharishi was creating the seat of the World Government of the Age of Enlightenment in Seelisberg. As part of this plan, the old Hotel Sonnenberg was to become the Capitol where often public meetings would be held in what was once the hotel's grand salon.

Quite early one morning, when most of the staff was still in their rooms asleep or meditating, I took my usual shortcut to breakfast, crossing the bridge from the Kulm to the Sonnenberg. On the bridge, which had a roof and windows on both sides, I stopped midway, to study the sample swatches for the exterior of the soon-to-be Capitol painted on the front of the Sonnenberg. I had narrowed my color choices to two when Maharishi surprised me from behind.

He greeted me sweetly. "Ah, it's my fastest designer," he smiled. Seeing what I was doing, he asked me which of the swatches I liked best. When I pointed out a creamy off-white one, he mentioned the goldenrod swatch beside it. "But isn't this one livelier?"

I knew he was not seeking an answer, but using the question for instruction. In my early-morning clarity of mind, it seemed that this was the root of the way TM people spoke. The language originated with Maharishi, where the question always included the answer.

At that moment, it seemed as if the swatches were painted on the building solely for this particular meeting with Maharishi and me. The word "livelier" jumped out at me. "Livelier" imbued the color with a lifelike quality. It wasn't the normal "too dark" or "light" or "too yellow or too red." Maharishi was showing me that a color could be "lively" as if it were alive with consciousness.

We discussed a few other swatches until I think he was convinced I understood that colors had more qualities than just their hue or light or darkness—they could be dull, or energetic—like any living thing.

Suddenly I felt Maharishi looking deep into me, he smiled as if he had discovered something, and said, "You have very subtle perception." It didn't appear to be a compliment; only a statement of fact, as he might have said, "You are tall." What he was telling me was something I already knew but usually was not in my awareness. His telling me immediately enlivened the perception—and I felt as if I'd been injected with a serum of bliss.

When our discussion of colors was complete, Maharishi said, "come" as he walked on towards the Sonnenberg. I caught up with him and, walking by his side, felt the power and grace of being in step with his gait. Together we headed into the old dining room, a huge space that had been used for storing old furniture from the hotel. Circular dining tables and wooden chairs covered with dust were stacked on top of each other. The room had the musty smell of years of disuse, but there was a feeling in the air that the space was about to be *enlivened*.

It was fun to watch Maharishi surveying the room as an architect or interior designer would, seeing beyond the clutter, envisioning its possibilities. His vision of that moment would slowly evolve into the assembly hall for the next phase of his plan for enlightening the world. In a few short months, with the help of skilled Swiss woodworkers, the room would resemble a true government assembly hall which would become the governing seat of Maharishi's worldwide movement. Maharishi's dais would be positioned against the inner wall facing the lake, with Mount Meru visible through floor-to-ceiling windows. Platforms would be built in a half-circle facing the dais, each one rising a step above the next in theater-like fashion. Along the front of each platform, there would be a waist-high natural wood wall, concealing a built-in counter behind which was space for each Governor of the Age of Enlightenment to sit.

But for now, Maharishi moved between the tables, chairs, and stacks of dishes and assorted leftovers from a bygone era. He began by talking to me alone, but quickly word spread among the staff and within fifteen minutes, the room was crowded with bleary-eyed members come to help. Maharishi reminded me of a commanding officer in the military, ordering the minions to toss broken chairs and tables out the open windows—seamlessly separating the junk from the savable antique furniture. Soon the junk became a growing pile on the street below.

My state of bliss from my earlier encounter with Maharishi remained. As I watched, I felt particularly close to him, having shared those precious moments. Over time, the symbolism of meeting him on the bridge occurred to me and grew in importance and eventually formed a conclusion: Maharishi had been helping me bridge the gap—the gap between the Relative world and the Absolute Field of Pure Consciousness.

Meanwhile Maharishi stood in a cloud of dust, so poised, so centered amid chaos. A room now filled with maybe fifty people were asking him questions, vying for his attention. Yet nothing shook him out of his natural state of consciousness. He pointed: *this chair goes, this table stays,* all the while giggling and smiling through the dust in total acceptance of everything.

I saw that he resisted nothing. Everything flowed around and through him like water down a stream. He was the stream bed allowing the flow to happen. And it all happened over him, around, and through him, so nothing was missed and everything was included.

In the end, it was as if nothing had ever happened at all. Consciousness itself was clearing the room of the old, making room for the new. Pure Consciousness was shifting from The Age of Ignorance into the coming Age of Enlightenment.

Someone poked me in the back. I was in the path of four or five staff who were carrying a table with a broken leg towards an open window.

"Take it, take it," Maharishi instructed them. "That one's old—we don't need old. Old is old, new is new."

He looked at me and laughed. In the moment, I knew he was confirming my conclusion. It happened within just an instant before he turned and walked away.

I added my hand to the group carrying the table. We took it to the window and with a count of "One, two, three!" sent it flying into the air and onto the pile on the street. I watched it shatter into pieces until it was no longer a table, and looked as if it never had been.

It was time for me to go. I walked out of the room and headed towards breakfast at the Waldhaus. It was a completely different scene in the dining room where I could see the Lila was in full swing being acted out there as if it were the next scene in my movie. Behind the counter a German server poured yogurt and muesli into the stainless serving vessels. The staff that hadn't been participating in the furniture purge in the Sonnenberg were lined up like cows waiting to be fed at a trough.

I lined up with them and joined the herd. Strangely, everyone I came in contact with seemed to have been transformed. The German servers were kinder and friendlier—and actually, performing their actions quite amenably.

So, this is how it worked! I heard Maharishi's words in my head, *"The world is as we are."*

A few days later, as I crossed the bridge on the way to breakfast, the painters had set up scaffolding and were busy painting the Sonnenberg a lively golden hue.

Meetings with the Master

For Maharishi's evening meetings, we would gather after dinner in the newly transformed dining room in the Sonnenberg. All the staff, the 108's, and the honored guests of the moment would be in attendance. The women's course leaders were often there as well, spirited away from their hotels on the lake in Maharishi's huge Daimler Benz.

As we awaited Maharishi's arrival, there would be a palpable sense of anticipation in the air lasting until the moment he finally entered, often an hour or more after the scheduled time. Then came an audible sigh of relief, *yes, he's finally here*, combined with the sentiment in everyone's heart that never waned, *what an absolute grace to be allowed to be in his presence.* This is not an exaggeration; this is the supreme reverence Maharishi evoked.

When he made his entrance and moved toward the stage,

197

Maharishi always seemed to be hidden inside an enveloping crowd, mostly visitors offering flowers or eager to hear an answer to a burning question. Arriving at the dais, he would gently kick off his sandals, unnoticed by most. A sizable painting of Guru Dev hung behind Maharishi's couch. Before sitting down, he would stop and stand for a long moment facing the portrait. Because of this gesture, I was sure Guru Dev was there with Maharishi attending the meeting.

Only then would Maharishi situate himself on the couch, adjusting his white silk dhoti as he crossed his legs, all the time surveying the audience to see who was in attendance. If there were long-time devotees, they would be seated in the front row at the foot of the dais. Maharishi might acknowledge one or more of them by exchanging a few words. Usually there were pandits in attendance seated on the dais on either side of Maharishi. He would turn to them, speak a few words in Hindi and they would begin to chant some Sanskrit verses from the Vedas. This was a signal for the few hundred or so of us in the hall to close our eyes and sink inside ourselves for a few minutes to ride the blissful wave of the pundit's voices.

Quietly in command, Maharishi would usually begin the meeting by turning his head to Vesey Creighton and say, "We should hear some good news today—mmh?" Vesey, in his patrician English manner, would step up to the podium on the dais, open a blue folder and read news of the Movement from around the world. He would tout successes from places far afield, sometimes mentioning the names of the people responsible. He might remark, "In Brazil, Benny has organized the initiation of five hundred people in a single day in Rio de Janeiro." After the news, Maharishi would start on a subject that might surprise everyone. It could be related to one of the topics Vesey brought up, or perhaps he'd invite a scientist to sit with him on stage, or he might give a discourse on a particular Veda. Nobody but Maharishi knew for sure the direction the meeting would take.

Regardless of the subject, the collective audience would almost instantly settle into a blissful calmness. The temperature in the room, even on the coldest nights, was always kept warm, as if we were sitting in front of a fireplace listening to grandfather tell a story. Our new chairs were so comfortable that sometimes it was a challenge to keep awake. The designers, as usual, had assigned seats near the front and a dropdown desktop for sketching layouts as Maharishi spoke. We were always ready for a topic to turn into a newsletter or brochure.

A good portion of the audience usually nodded off, especially the honored elders in the front row. Maharishi never seemed to mind whether someone was awake or asleep, and I had the feeling that his message got through no matter what a person's state. But if you were alert enough to follow along, you would be astonished by the brilliance of his words. Luckily, there were three video cameramen recording his talk in a mobile control room housed in a Mercedes truck parked outside.

Sometimes Maharishi would stop at a salient point and take a few questions from the audience. It was always an inspiration to see someone able to follow the train of Maharishi's thoughts. But, for me, simply being in the Master's presence was all that mattered. Strangely, magically, beautifully, finally, in the decades after my being in Seelisberg, Maharishi's knowledge still surfaces in me. The more my consciousness has expanded over time, the more I have understood. His knowledge appears to me when I am able to absorb it.

The meetings often felt like celebrations. Over time, gold curtains became the backdrop for Maharishi's stage and over the windows in the rear. Flags of every country were hung from the ceiling and more and more vases of flowers proliferated around Maharishi. Under the bright video lights, the stage and the room eventually resembled a concert venue—a concert of classical Indian musicians playing, of course, in a palace. Maharishi loved music, and there was always some available. Rick Stanley and several women performed songs often extoling the Movement's recent successes. The traditional ending to the day's festivities were verses of the Sama Veda sung by the pandits.

Maharishi would depart the hall first, while the audience stood with palms pressed together, thanking him for allowing us the grace of being in his darshan. On the way to my room in the Kulm, a few doors down from Maharishi's, I was in the habit of counting the shoes left outside his door by the people invited inside. I joked to myself that the number of shoes equaled the seriousness of the meeting. I also joked that if my consciousness was more developed, I would know who belonged with each pair.

The Razor-thin Path

As I watched the seasons change in Seelisberg the more I felt blessed to be there. I became filled with joy at simply being. Each new day under Maharishi's umbrella filled me with gratitude for the privilege of being able to stroll through the magical forests. In winter, I wore my beautiful new suit beneath a blue wool overcoat, with a tan scarf wrapped around my neck. There were moments, so complete, they were all there was and ever would be. I experienced Seelisberg existing as a world all its own, outside the constraints of space and time. Somehow, the ship that was Seelisberg with me on board had slipped through the doorway into Infinity, where cosmic bliss washed over anyone standing on deck.

One autumn day, as I floated beneath the trees after rain, the sun poked through the veil of mist, illuminating drops of water on the branches. The dripping water splashed me with bits of cosmic light. Yet, something surfaced, reminding me that I was treading a razor-thin path balanced by an opposing force on the other side.

The forest trail I followed ended at a sheer cliff dropping more than a thousand feet to the lake. This time, as I stopped to stare down into the black void below, a shiver ran up my spine and vibrated throughout my body—and I felt as afraid as I ever had in the jungles of Vietnam. The fear froze me so solidly in place that I was unable to move my feet. I felt there was no escape and I was staring into the womb of death. I had come right to the edge where beyond it nothing existed. Beyond the cliff was the end of this world and everything in it. I knew that whatever held me there was teaching me a lesson, but I feared it might force me over the edge. It might want me to jump. I saw myself plummeting down the rock cliff, my overcoat like a pair of folded wings, sending me ever faster into this death dive.

With superhuman effort—I believed was a matter of life and death—I lifted my leg, moved my foot, turned my body around—and fled in the other direction. I felt compelled to hurry faster and faster until I reached the end of the forest, to a place where I could see the sun sparkling on the wet road. To a place where I would be safe.

Heading back to the Capital, I thought about where this sense of danger might have come from. I wondered what had punctured the bubble of bliss I had been floating in? I should not have been surprised. I was learning from Maharishi that we must strive to live according to the Laws of Nature. But Nature's Laws, he said, require balance. For every action there must be an equal and opposite reaction. As I walked toward my office I concluded that the level of bliss I was feeling, demanded an equal portion of the opposite. Good and evil, bliss and fear, positive and negative, these dualities, are the undercurrent of our lives and to maintain balance we must navigate between the two. The further we progress spiritually, I'd heard Maharishi say, the narrower the path between the two becomes until, finally, we must traverse this razor-thin line with extreme care. If we are not vigilant, a fall can be the consequence. Maharishi's teachings had given me the knowledge, and this experience, this utterly frightening moment on the cliff's edge, gave me a more complete understanding.

Spotting the Capital buildings brought me into a more balanced sense of being. Entering the Pilgerheim brought a smile to my face because I knew I could retreat once again into a world where I felt safe—behind my drawing board in the small office shared with Eike. I said nothing about the incident to him, but afterward, I better understood his fear of straying too far from the shelter of Maharishi's protection. Living in the rarified, subtle atmosphere of Seelisberg, many of the staff were fearful of the harsh environment of the outside world.

Ha — Infinity!

As I became more immersed in Maharishi's teachings, my ability to transcend what had been known as my own individual reality became deeper and broader. I had a chance for further progress when Maharishi offered a six-month course in the French Alps. The subject was rumored to be an experiment in unlocking the ancient secrets of the Siddhis, known in common parlance as superpowers.

I arrived in Avoriaz, a ski resort in part of the Mont Blanc massif, the largest in the Alps, which meant, upon arrival, that it was time for a trek. It was the end of summer so there was no snow on the mountain's gentle slope above our hotel. It rose up a few thousand feet to a series of sharp granite cliffs known as *Les Dents* because they resembled teeth. An hour or so of easy hiking brought me and a few others to the top of the tall pillars. Beyond them, a sheer granite ledge dropped down for a mile or more into a deep green valley. It was one of the most expansive and breathtaking views I had ever witnessed. Although it was sunny on the climb up, a huge bank of billowy clouds gathered a few thousand feet above. It seemed like someone had pushed a huge gray and white structure overhead.

I knew how quickly the weather can change in the mountains and I felt something ominous approaching. When I mentioned this to the others, they were so enthralled with the scenery, that they seemed unconcerned. Unable to convince anyone, I headed back down on my own to the hotel. I felt small and powerless descending on the back of such a giant mountain with huge clouds crowding the sky above me. The clouds had turned a dark bluish-gray and were lowering as if the sky were falling. In no time, the bottoms of the clouds completely enveloped the mountain making visibility almost zero. Without warning, the clouds lit up from their insides with dramatic flashes of light accompanied by deafening drumbeats of thunder. Everyone on the mountain was caught inside a lightning storm from which there was no escape.

I tucked myself into a small crevasse in a ledge of rocks while the storm released its fury. There was no other option; the storm raged like an angry god mercilessly shaking the mountain. The temperature dropped, the flashes grew brighter and the thunder deafening. Then, as if things couldn't get any wilder, marble-sized hailstones dropped out of the sky blanketing the rocky ground in ice. This went on for a few long minutes until, as quickly as the storm began, it reached a finale with a series of silent electric flashes that lit up everything.

As the sky cleared, I watched the other climbers stumble down the mountainside in the distance. The temperature had dropped twenty degrees or more. Gathering back at the hotel, as it turned out, the other climbers hadn't fared well. Several of them had been struck by sheet lightning and had burns on their skin where metal necklaces and wristwatches had electrified.

The storm appeared to be a bad omen—and indeed it was. When Maharishi arrived a day later, he intensely disliked Avoriaz. He declared that the town looked to be a failed experiment in architecture with all the structures purposely created with random angles and no straight lines anywhere. Instead of being a pleasant-looking village that melded organically into the environment, the result was visual confusion. There was hardly a flat surface anywhere to provide visual rest. In his way of getting to the point, Maharishi said the town must have been designed by hippies.

Within days, the course was on a plane flying with Maharishi to Biarritz, an elegant resort town bordering Spain on the Atlantic coast. The buildings, mostly from another century, were designed with style and grace. It was a place where the "new me" belonged. Dressed in my new suit, I stood straighter as I strolled through town, often on the way to the only five-star bakery in France outside Paris.

Our course was held in two hotels on the best beach in Biarritz—the extraordinary Le Palais and the elegant but less over-the-top Miramar. Maharishi resided in Le Palais but his talks were held in the Miramar's palatial dining room. At the start of the course, his couch and dais were set up so that his back was to the ocean, which was ominously visible through the floor-to-ceiling windows behind him. This positioning, to me, was unsettling and even frightening at times, especially during those dark days when clouds threatened and winds whipped up large waves on the Atlantic. It felt much more comfortable when Maharishi moved to the other side of the room facing the sea.

Biarritz, known for being on France's stormiest section of coastline, seemed a fitting venue for Maharishi to be unlocking the secrets of ancient texts and describing the supernatural powers contained in the ancient Vedic literature. We might not have known it at the start, but we were participating in history being made.

Maharishi went as deep as the texts went, parsing each sentence, each word, even each letter and the meaning of its sound. It was extraordinary to witness. I wondered, who is this great sage? And how am I even allowed to be in his divine presence? I had no answers to these questions. I was both overwhelmed and honored to be in the presence of this amazing teacher reclaiming knowledge that had remained hidden for far too long. It was like standing behind someone with a golden key watching him open an ancient door locked for centuries. Each day, he would open another door.

As usual, I was quickly lost in the jungle of thoughts and words. Once again, I confirmed for myself, that I was not an intellectual who could easily understand the fine points of texts as Maharishi revealed them. Instead, I experienced a scholarly overload that puzzled my mind and left me helpless in my seat. I was saved only by the soothing sounds of Maharishi's voice washing over me, sometimes in cadence with the waves breaking outside on the beach.

I suppose because by then I was considered a dedicated member of International Staff, I earned a seat up front among the honored guests and scientists. This put me in Maharishi's direct line of sight, as well as afforded me space beneath the umbrella of his darshan. When Maharishi and I made eye contact, it seemed he was communicating with me alone. Although I might not have been on the same intellectual level as those around me, on a *non-verbal* level I knew I was as in-tune with Maharishi as anyone. It was happening more and more that Maharishi answered a question the instant it arose in my mind.

Maharishi often entered the hall during the meditation that began each meeting. I almost always opened my eyes when I sensed him walking in. Brahmachary Nandkishore would rush to the couch to place Maharishi's deerskin.

Maharishi settled onto his deerskin, pulling his tan cashmere shawl around him, while he surveyed the people in front of him. Sitting as close as I was, I watched the subtle changes in his expression as his eyes moved around the room—a slight smile here, a flicker of annoyance there. Sometimes even a question mark would appear on his forehead. To me, he was at the center of the Cosmos. Seeing him, pulled me down and in—back to my unbounded Self—much like the mantra in meditation.

Once, during the meditation when our eyes were supposed to be closed, he caught me with my eyes open looking at him. First, I felt the recognition of being caught, followed by a flash of love, freely given, despite my supposed disobedience. Contained within that love was the recognition that it was perfectly okay to be myself, and not beholden to any concept that could be considered right or wrong. I realized that within finer levels of existence, there are no opposites.

Patanjali's Yoga Sutras tells us that in the highest state of consciousness, Brahman, there really are no rules, such as right or wrong. In Brahman, everything is self-referral, a totality. Being part of Maharishi's totality included being a bit mischievous, like he was.

There were times when I couldn't decide whether Maharishi was looking inside or outside himself. Although his eyes were open, and he might even be looking around the room, it seemed as if he was gazing at something in a far distant place. But at other times, his gaze appeared to reveal more than that. As if he were fully involved in some inner scenario. As if he were watching a scene in the Lila playing somewhere else, his body and the room we were in proving no distraction at all.

Sometimes I felt as if I slipped into Maharishi's state of consciousness by mistake. I would experience what was going on within him and would feel connected to what he was connected to. It had nothing to do with what he might be talking about at the moment; it was on a much subtler plane than language. In these moments, I realized that the humble Indian sage in the white dhoti was much, much more than just a man, he was a slice of the Infinite.

But Maharishi took no credit for anything that might make him seem to be a great soul. As he went about enlightening the world, one person at a time, he continually gave thanks to Guru Dev for any achievements. By doing this, Maharishi was not only honoring his beloved teacher, but connecting with the Holy Tradition of Masters. Undoubtedly, the power I felt sitting in front of me was transmitted through an invisible cord that connected me to him and he to Guru Dev and the great masters in our tradition.

Further back in time, following the line from Guru Dev, was Adi Shankara, the first great monk of the tradition. But the cord continued even further back to Lord Shiva, perhaps the most powerful of the Hindu Gods. Maharishi's connection with Shiva was the connection with the Infinite. Maharishi's full title is *Maharishi Mahesh Yogi*—and *Mahesh* in Sanskrit, is *Shiva*. It was probably these undeniably powerful connections that brought the great relief I felt that first time I meditated. The relief felt so cosmically deep I knew it couldn't be contained in just this one lifetime. It had been felt before.

At times, as I witnessed myself sitting in a royal ballroom in the Hotel Miramar in the south of France, I would know that I too, was part of this eternal chain of events. I could smell the dirt on the floor of the ashram in the Himalayas where Guru Dev sat and gave darshan. And, beyond that, I sat at Shankara's feet. And even beyond that, I was part of the Divine infinite nature of Shiva.

Maharishi was the embodiment of the Infinite in this lifetime. *And so was I.* This most fulfilling realization came to me as I peered through the ultimate veil of illusion, the Maya.

I knew that having this connection to the Holy Tradition of Masters was the greatest blessing a person could have. What an indescribable comfort it was to know that I was part of what was right with the world and the cosmos. Being connected to the masters meant being part of the Eternal Everything. It also meant that those around me were part of it, as well. As I looked around the room, I was certain that they felt this connection, too. This made me feel that the members of the course and I were the most important group of beings on the planet at this time. After all, we were here for one reason only—to help Maharishi achieve his grand vision of ending suffering on Earth. I was part of his Movement. I was connected to it as much as anyone. Once again, I remembered that I was a slice of infinite Pure Consciousness Maharishi called "That." If the Relative world—the one we can see, hear, smell, taste, and touch—is "this" then the Infinite, Unchanging, Unbounded, Unified field, can only be called "That" with a capital "T."

One day Maharishi gave a particularly intense talk about developing the more advanced siddhis. The "extraordinary powers" are gained with additional practices based on transcending in meditation. In Maharishi's eyes, the siddhis are a person's birthright. What the world would consider "extraordinary" should be ordinary. He said that people called what he was doing "impossible," and he joked that yes, we relish being impossible. We are all about accomplishing the impossible.

His talk began in the morning and continued through the day until late in the afternoon, leaving me exhausted from trying to keep up—all the while knowing I never could. I was convinced that Maharishi exhausted our minds on purpose; with the mind shut down consciousness had the space to shine through.

Near the end of his talk, Maharishi gave us a technique to use following our meditations that evening, and he wanted us to share the resulting experiences with him in the next day's meeting. This felt exciting because, although he didn't say as much, it seemed he was using us to verify a theory. We were part of his noble experiment. After Maharishi had left the hall, we all filed out silently on our way to our rooms to meditate. Crowded in front of the elevators, everyone was so filled with bliss that not a word was heard. The silence was so profound, not a word *could* be spoken.

Opening the door to my suite, I was filled with extreme gratitude simply because of the beauty of it. The anteroom had a large antique desk. There was a huge bed with a padded headboard covered in silk that filled much of the bedroom. At the far end, double doors opened onto a balcony overlooking the beach and the ocean. I unlatched the doors, and the gauzy curtains swept into the room like a benevolent spirit riding a wave of salty air. It was winter and off-season so the beach below was deserted. The sun had already disappeared, so with no horizon, the sea and sky seemed as one. I stood thinking about how far away from my old world I was. And that I wouldn't give up this new existence for anything. I was amazed. I had never been so fulfilled. I had everything I ever wanted and lacked for nothing. Even this huge suite fit for a king felt just right.

Before starting my meditation, I sat down on the edge of the bed and tossed some loose change from my pocket onto the bedside table along with my wallet and room key. In my state of what I would call *pure openness*, I was astounded when I glanced over at what I had carelessly tossed on the table. The collection of simple objects—a wallet, some coins, and a key—displayed the totality of existence. It was all right there contained in the objects themselves and the position each object had taken relative to the others. It had been a random toss without any predetermination, without trying to control anything. As a result, it mirrored the perfection of existence. Not only that, but in addition to the objects themselves, my glance at the objects, were both included in this profound reality.

I was aware of how blessed I was to be given a glimpse into creation as a Unified Whole where any one thing—including any action—is common to everything else in existence. I saw that there is no difference between things and actions, that everything is energy—energy connected to me—the same energy I am made of. All material things making up "the grand illusion" of the Relative World are connected. A person, a wallet, a wristwatch, a toss of coins, the toss itself, even a thought about the toss—all are connected. There is nothing that isn't part of The Whole.

"All this is That."

Perhaps most profound of all was knowing that I was part of it as well. There was no separation between my consciousness and Pure Consciousness itself. I was nothing but consciousness. I was no longer just a localized being on a course in Biarritz, I was Biarritz, I was the course. My consciousness included everything. There was nothing that was not included.

I eagerly climbed onto the huge bed, propped myself up with several king size pillows against the cushioned headboard, and drifted into meditation. My meditation began by my sinking into a deep sea, followed by rising back up to the surface, like a diver coming up for air. I rode a huge swell on the surface of the sea before sinking again into Pure Consciousness, the field containing the universality of all things. As often is the case, I knew I had experienced it before. It felt so familiar, and I knew it to be the only place there is and *ever* was. I was like a fish being tossed back into the sea. Its home.

I had felt the same thing when I was a child when I used to lie in the field behind our house transfixed by a single blade of grass moving in the wind. The blade would become so beautiful I would fall into an inescapable ecstasy, realizing that the blade was an integral part of the infinite creation. And, in fact, the infinite creation was encompassed in the blade of grass.

Now in this hotel, I pressed my eyes closed with a feeling of gratitude. When I next checked my watch, I saw that almost two hours had passed, and I felt as if I had just closed my eyes. So, there was no space or time.

Ha infinity!

River of Love

There was being on staff, and then there was taking a course—they each had their advantages. In Seelisberg, my evolution felt faster, being in the presence of the Master day and night, which in comparison, made being on a course seem restful and easy. As a participant on an advanced course, in contrast to being on staff with Maharishi, I was free of distraction. All that was necessary was to follow a simple routine that made life unfold effortlessly. Exactly what one experiences during six months of rounding is difficult to put into words. A great deal can be achieved from doing very little or, what many would say, doing nothing at all. During a course, on the surface, the days become habitual. We wake, clean up, do asanas, pranayama, meditate, rest, then do it all over again the next day. The very strictness of the routine is key. It creates a place where you never have to think about what you are doing.

That's the joy of it all—it's no longer in the mind.

My opportunity to be on another course showed up when word floated through Seelisberg that Maharishi was giving a course in the late spring and summer in Arosa, a ski resort in the Alps. I was certainly primed and ready. After receiving Maharishi's permission to go, I boarded a train for Zurich and from there to Chur where passengers to Arosa transferred to a narrow-gauge railway that climbed along a rushing river into the Alps. I got off at the last stop, arriving in another version of heaven, a charming village of chalets clustered around a small lake. The snow had melted and the mountains surrounding the town were bright green dotted with white edelweiss.

I was assigned to the Hotel Eden tucked into a forested hillside above the town near the ski lifts. Typically Swiss, it was stark, clean and comfortable, and lacking any real charm. My room had a single bed with a few sturdy pieces of wooden furniture. But a balcony overlooked a river valley between two mountains and the view was spectacular.

The first week before the inevitable exhaustion set in, I explored the countryside and trekked across the meadows enjoying the flowers and the warmth of the sun. High up a mountain, I came across a small pond of clear water ringed with mud and dung, with deep hoof prints of cows. With no one around, I stripped off my clothes and dove into the frigid water. I had heard that the icy plunge is beneficial in maintaining celibacy. Skinny-dipping alone on a mountain made me feel like a true *sannyasin*, an ascetic who sheds all worldly concerns.

The course began as others, with rounds of meditation and

yoga. While meditation gave me more energy, rounding, along with its intense release of stress, was always exhausting. We were quickly given a full rounding schedule: meditation and asanas from morning to night with a two-hour break for lunch and walk-and-talk. An MD from New Zealand, who was there to guide us through a thirty-day cleansing fast, extolled the value of ridding the body of toxins by depriving it of solid food and cleansing it with enemas. On his regimen, we progressed rapidly from the normal course diet of rice and cooked vegetables, to a liquid green concoction, called Bieler's Broth, made with a liquified blend of zucchini, string beans, celery, and parsley. After a week or so we transitioned to fruit juice and from that, to only bottled spring water with a grapefruit or lemon juice chaser. The doctor taught us the enema process which we were expected to do at least once a day. The effects on the body and mind were drastic. After a few days everyone was incredibly spaced out and it only got worse after that. Two weeks into the fast we were all feeling so weak we were hardly talking, spending most of our time in our rooms rounding and flushing out toxins.

Rounding, in addition to the fasting, put me in a unique state of mind. I was floating in outer space without being tethered to a spaceship. Since maintaining silence was part of this course routine, I glided through my day without speaking, feeling the deep stillness all around me. At times, there were ecstatic moments of pure bliss.

The only time we were encouraged to talk was when we were asked to describe our experiences to Maharishi, either by speakerphone or in person, when he was visiting. We were given paper forms each evening to detail that day's experiences. For the most part, my experiences were within the normal range for the course—waves of bliss at times during meditation, crystal-clear vision during waking hours with moments of joy—but nothing out of the ordinary.

Until late one night.

I awakened from deep sleep to witness something my mind couldn't believe. With my head still on the pillow, I opened my eyes and my room was as bright as if the lights were on. The air all around me was thick, filled with swirling sparkling golden particles of light. The particles were so thick in the air that when I sat up I made a tunnel. Then I saw the particles were in motion, flowing as a river towards and out the open door to the balcony.

I climbed out of bed in awe. Transfixed by the silence, I moved through the thick air and stepped out onto the balcony where I witnessed something even more astonishing. Streams of the same sparkling substance flowed from all the windows in our hotel. It was as if the Eden Hotel was a giant watering pot, pouring golden light from all its rooms. Out in front of the hotel, some distance away, the individual streams joined together to form a river that flowed through the valley between two mountains and on out into the universe.

I went back inside, sat down at my desk and wrote about what I was seeing while I was still seeing it, while the air was still thick with gold.

I wrote that I was witnessing a river of love flowing from the heart of each meditator in the Eden Hotel. I knew it was love because it could be felt as well as seen. And I knew that our group was healing the world with a balm of the most powerful substance in creation. What I named "love" was in actuality the finest of all the building blocks of creation—finer even than sub-atomic particles. It could also be called "bliss." The meditators in our hotel were creating the glue, the energy, that held the cosmos together. We were healing our planet and all Creation by supplying the substance of which it was formed.

Sometime later I realized that I had experienced what Maharishi had been telling us. A few years hence, it was to become known as "The Maharishi Effect." When a group is transcending together, the effect is exponentially magnified. I had seen, first hand, that Maharishi's words were true beyond any doubt.

It is one thing to hear about something that seems impossible and quite another to witness it for yourself.

I took it as a positive sign that my experience of bliss in meditation was being validated in the Relative World. Still, I am a realist, so I believe in practical proof. What is the point of having celestial experiences in meditation only? We should be able to have the same experience with our eyes open, which is the way we spend ninety percent of our day. Maharishi assured us that our practices had great benefits for our lives, and he is undoubtedly the most practical being I have ever known.

As far back as teacher training in La Antilla, I recall Maharishi talking about this. He said that the Relative—the material world, experienced by the senses—is imbued with the Absolute Field of Pure Consciousness and eventually, the two shall meet. When the two worlds meet in our consciousness, anything becomes possible, and life is experienced without boundaries.

This was the knowledge behind the experience: That Pure Consciousness makes up the substance of Creation, of the Relative World. So, on a subtle level, while acting in the world I should be at one with nature. In a sense, any action of "mine" is really Mother Nature Herself acting. Still, I was looking for proof—which, as always, appeared when I least expected it.

The atmosphere in Arosa was sublimely still. The silence imbued in the stillness was palpable. My walk-and-talks took me along a path that wove through the forest behind the hotel. I always brought along a pocket full of muesli to feed the birds who, unlike most Swiss, were anything but reserved. They became used to seeing me each day after lunch dropping pieces of cereal along the path. They would follow above me in the trees, fluttering from branch to branch, every so often daring to dive down to pick up a bit of the cereal off the ground. I wondered if they would eat from my hand, so one day I stood still and held out my arm with a handful of muesli. One brave bird tried a quick grab-and-go but was so nervous it missed taking any food. He tried a second time and was successful. Finding that no harm occurred, he made the trip several times. The other birds witnessed what was happening and soon others were diving down and eating out of my hand.

How blissful to have gained the trust of birds! Feeling them grip the side of my hand with a pinch of their tiny talons connected me with the animal kingdom. That trust broke through the boundary of "them" and "me," *proof* that we were living the Unified Wholeness Maharishi talked about. The birds and I were fellow creatures sharing the same planet—equals in God's eyes.

All was right with the world. Everything was just as it should be.

Flying

Back to work in Seelisberg, we heard of Maharishi's desire to deepen the knowledge of his followers. A wonderful example of Maharishi's great genius was his creation of the siddhis program, the supernormal powers outlined in Patanjali's Yoga Sutras, one of the most profound Indian manuscripts. There was a buzz of excitement in the air because participants were, in a sense, volunteering to be test-pilots. The first siddhis course containing instructions for the "Flying Sutra" was to be held in private in Seelisberg because Maharishi knew that yogic "flying" would attract the press and could easily be misunderstood as a novelty. Although International Staff members were not invited, we quickly learned that the meditation program, including the practice of flying, took place in a meeting room behind closed doors, of course covered with sheets. German guards stood on either side to prevent prying eyes. After a few days, however, the guards were often missing so it was easy for curious staff like me to pull back the corner of a sheet and peer in. I saw about two dozen meditators scattered about the room with eyes closed and legs folded, seated cross-legged in full or half-lotus positions. The floor was covered from wall to wall with mattresses, sheets neatly tucked over them.

Every so often one of the meditators, sitting cross-legged on a mattress, would *hop*. Then another would do the same, and another and another, until a kind of collective hopping mania overtook the group. The hopping appeared to be contagious. A few stragglers were either late to join in or didn't catch the mania at all. This didn't look like flying to me, but it looked so interesting, that I didn't want to miss out.

Fortunately, another siddhis course was announced on the heels of the first and this time I made sure I would be allowed to attend. Maharishi approved, and once again, I was off to Arosa and the Hotel Eden.

Rounding commenced as usual—and courses were actually seeming to be just that, *usual.*

After a few days, once we had settled in, Maharishi arrived from Seelisberg by helicopter to instruct us in the siddhis. We had heard so much about these superhuman abilities, but none of us was certain about what they were and how we would perform them. Having Maharishi impart the siddhis in person was infinitely powerful. In their own way they were just as powerful as receiving my mantra back in Westwood Village, ages ago.

When I arrived for my first flying session, I was as excited as the first time I drove a car. I came down to the meeting room bursting with anticipation and found everything transformed. The room was filled from end to end with foam mattresses covered with white sheets just as I had seen in Seelisberg. I walked a little unsteadily across the foam and settled into my favorite corner to begin my meditation with the others. Our instructions were to start the practice of our sutras after our normal twenty-minute meditation. When it became time for the last—the much-anticipated Flying Sutra—I followed Maharishi's instructions.

And, nothing happened.

I meditated a little more, then tried again.

Nothing.

Oh yes, I thought, like meditation—no trying allowed. Again, this time with hardly any effort.

Nada.

Nothing happened. No sensation of lightness. Certainly, no sensation of flying.

I opened my eyes to a surprise. A few people were hopping! Some were shaking slightly as if in preparation for hopping. Others were grunting and some were laughing out loud.

Again, I closed my eyes.

Mmmm—I felt a warm feeling overcome me. A sense of wellbeing. Yet nothing else was happening—not until I opened my eyes again and was amazed to find that, *without even knowing it*, I had moved. Miraculously. I was a foot away from where I had been. I had felt no sensations, no lifting off the ground, no settling down. I had gotten *here* from *there*—without effort.

This, then, was a *siddhi*, a magical power. Superhuman? I

wasn't sure. I wasn't at all sure what had taken place. But I knew this was the experience of something happening *without doing*.

I had done nothing to make it happen.

Night on the Mountain

*B*ack in Seelisberg, I perceived, more and more, the intense beauty of my surroundings. On sunny days following a snowfall, the sun would crystalize, melting snow and dressing the village in elegant jewelry made of ice. But as much as I appreciated living in the midst of such splendor, my mind kept returning to the siddhis. Practical by nature, I had an overwhelming desire to apply the super-human powers we had learned, into my normal existence. I felt the power of the siddhis like prowling tigers lurking behind me ready to pounce. I could feel their breath, but longed to be bitten by their power, but didn't yet know how to summon them.

They appeared when I least expected them.

I had been wanting to explore the mountain behind the Capital, to climb farther up the trail than I had gone, so one morning, I packed a bag of muesli, nuts, and raisins, a bottle of water and a Lindt chocolate bar. For the first leg of the journey, I planned to stop at the bench by the overlook to meditate, and then head farther up the mountain into unexplored territory. However, when I reached the bench, I was so invigorated that stopping seemed out of the question. Instead, I bit into the chocolate bar and set out again through the forest.

Melting snow from the sun had formed an icy crust on the trail, which may have looked spectacular, but made for slow climbing. The hard rubber soles of my boots were extra slippery on the ice. But the moment I started to feel sorry for myself about the difficulty of trekking, an elderly gentleman in Lederhosen came waltzing down the trail as sure-footed as if the mountain didn't exist. He greeted me with a pipe clenched in his teeth, red-faced and smiling. After seeing him and making the necessary attitude adjustment, I continued up through the forest without complaint.

Not long after, the trail emerged from the dark trees into a sunny snow-covered meadow. On the far side of the field, a small log hut was tucked under some pines. The scene was almost too precious to believe. Although I had never been there, it appeared so familiar that I felt as if I was looking backward into the past. Perhaps I had seen it in a fairytale. I was in Switzerland, after all, the land of Heidi and Rumpelstiltskin.

There were no footprints crossing the meadow to the hut, so I assumed it was deserted. Curious to find out, I started across sinking into the much softer snow. Because of the unusual stillness of the meadow, I was super-conscious of my surroundings. The closer I came, the surer I was that the hut was empty. It also seemed like a very special and powerful place, which made me feel like an intruder in a foreign land. I had traveled only a few miles from the hectic buzzing of the Capital, yet I was in a different world entirely, as if the scene had changed in my movie.

When I stepped up onto the hut's covered porch, I was suddenly chilled by dampness. I stood in the penetrating quiet, certain that the cabin was unoccupied and had been for some time. I knocked on the door anyway, then lifted the latch and pushed the door open to a wave of dank, cold air. The hut was spare inside, with a built-in platform bed taking up one wall. A gray wool blanket was neatly folded on a mattress with a striped feather pillow resting on top. Against the far wall, was a small cast iron stove with some shelves beside it. On the top shelf were a cooking pot and a frying pan, a few pieces of silverware, a single plate and a bowl. The shelf below held some cans of soup, vegetables, and meat.

I guessed the hut was a refuge for shepherds to spend a chilly summer night while their sheep grazed in the meadow. Three logs were stacked in a pyramid inside the stove with crumpled newspaper and some wood shavings underneath. A box of wooden matches sat on the counter. I lit the newspaper and sat back on the bed to pull off my boots. As much as I loved the boots, they were heavy on my feet and had caused blisters on my toes. Glad to be free of them, I laid back on the bed and pulled the blanket over me. I intended to nap for a few minutes and then continue hiking up the mountain. But the burning wood in the stove quickly heated the small room with a pleasing pine scent and I drifted off to the soporific ticking sound of the iron stove heating up. When I woke, after what I thought had been only a few minutes, the fire was out and the cabin was cold. I couldn't believe my watch read 9:15, which meant that I had slept for more than ten hours! When I opened the door, I looked up into a pitch-black sky filled with a sheet of stars.

I couldn't remember when I had felt so rested. Or, strangely, so content. Standing on the porch, I breathed in the frozen air beneath the boundless sky. My body felt weightless, completely transparent. I seemed infinite—Unbounded Pure Consciousness itself. I felt as amazing and transcendent as I had following my first ever meditation in California.

Then my mind intruded with a flood of thoughts. First, it was very cold and dark and I was somewhere deep in the forest alone. I wasn't frightened as I had been in Vietnam where enemies lurked in the forest. Still, I felt lost in space and didn't want to remain there for another minute. I thought it would be nearly impossible to find my way back to Seelisberg in the dark without a flashlight. It hadn't been easy to get where I'd climbed for several miles through a forest with a snow-covered floor.

An owl screeched in a nearby tree.

I knew I could heat the cabin and stay the night. But suddenly, I had an overwhelming desire to return to the safety of the "Mother Ship."

I became a soldier again and assessed my situation. Scanning the edges of the forest, I searched across the meadow for the place where the trail had brought me here.

What happened next was astounding. Without moving, I found myself up in the starry sky looking down at myself standing on the porch of the hut. Only, what was looking down at myself was not me. It was Pure Consciousness witnessing the person I thought I was.

The snow-covered meadow glowed in the starlight.

Again, I heard the owl's screech, but this time I saw her seated on a tree branch across the side of the meadow. She was showing me the entrance to the trail.

I laughed.

I tidied up the cabin and picked up my boots from in front of the cold stove. The leather had softened and the boots were warm when I pulled them on. I watched myself zip up my parka and head outside latching the door behind me. I was ready to descend the mountain.

I followed my footprints, visible as shadows in the snow until I started down the trail. There the dense canopy of trees in the forest blocked out the night sky. At first the trail was hidden in the dark. But I had the support of Nature that Maharishi talked about. And more than that, now that I *was* Pure Consciousness, I *was* Nature. My *thoughts* had the power to make things happen.

When I *thought* of the need to see more clearly, *the path illuminated.* Here, alone in the dark, without a witness, *I embodied the magical power of a siddhi, the ability to create light.*

I had to laugh.

I thought, someday I should write about this.

Then I thought, no one would believe it.

In no time, I passed the bench at the familiar overlook. Beneath me, bordering the lake, were the familiar streetlights and headlights from cars twinkling in the dark. The intensely beautiful view begged me to stop and take it all in. Now, I understood why I was so enamored with the view from my room in the Kulm. I understood why the cars and the trains going through Mount Meru, zooming in and out of the tunnel, always seemed so magical. It was magical because it was all happening *in* me. The whole scene, in fact, the entire world, was inside me. Because I was unbounded—infinite in every respect—I was the magician creating the magic, creating Creation.

Shivering, I thought of my warm room and snug bed. A kind of magical momentum pulled me forward, bringing me home. The rest of the way down the mountain I was in a state of total bliss *just having the thought* of the welcoming safety of Maharishi's holy sanctuary.

Back in my room, finished with the long trek, I wasn't one bit tired. It seemed like my hike up the mountain and back had taken place in no time at all.

I was not even sure that it had even happened.

Silent Night

*O*nce something is experienced, it cannot be unexperienced.
Being with Maharishi, I began to witness life on a deeper
level and understood that everything exists within a field of silent
stillness existing *in us* and *all around us.* The Pure Consciousness
we experience in meditation exists within that field when we
transcend the thinking mind, but we don't often experience it in
the waking state outside of meditation when the eyes are open.
But once I knew it was there at all times in front of me as well as
inside me, life was never quite the same.

The world looked different, imbued by a golden substance
that made everything seem intensely beautiful. Trees in the
forest contained a glow from inside proclaiming that they were
conscious beings. Walking up the road out of town, I would often
lean against a fence staring at the cows as they munched on the

grass. In my new awareness, the grass had become greener, and the cows more cow-like. Looking into their eyes, they seemed almost human and I wondered how I had never noticed this before. It was no wonder that in India cows are considered holy.

I thought back to the morning I met Maharishi on the bridge between the hotels, when he mentioned refined perception. I realized that his telling me had been the *knowledge*; now I was having the *experience*. Or, really, it seemed more like the experience was embracing me because I had very little to do with making it happen. Viewing what was happening in another way, I was experiencing what Maharishi had been telling us all along: that Pure Consciousness likes to invade the Relative. It seemed to me that it was slowly seeping in through the membrane of the seen world.

On one Christmas Eve in Seelisberg, Pure Consciousness made itself known beautifully and undeniably. Some friends invited me to a Christmas Eve Mass in the nearby village of Emmetten, a place I had never been to and always wanted to see. It was said to be an ancient village of stone buildings perched on a mountain.

Traveling in the Citroen, just as it was beginning to snow, we climbed a road of switchbacks even higher into the mountains. Upon first sight, Emmetten appeared even more magical than I had imagined. Because the streets were too narrow for cars, we parked on the outskirts of town at the base of the town's steep hill. While falling snowflakes turned to gold under the streetlights, we walked on cobblestone streets, following people as they made their way to the church. At the highest point in the village, the stone church stood out brightly lit against the deep blue of the sky. We had entered a scene in a fairytale. A priest, a plump and red-faced Santa Claus, stood on the church steps welcoming us in Swiss accented English.

The church inside was warm and inviting. It was decorated with a Christmas tree on one side of the altar and a nativity scene, surrounded with red and white flowers, on the other. My friends chose to sit together in the rear. I took a seat up front in the second row, but then noticed that the pews there were filling up with women all dressed in black, their faces covered with veils, the town widows. I gave up my seat and moved to a side aisle where a thoughtful family scrunched themselves together and waved to me to sit with them. It was an innocent expression of kindness that made me feel I was part of their family. Until then I hadn't realized that I missed my parents and my sister and longed to spend the holiday at home. Suddenly my heart opened and filled with the true spirit of Christmas.

The priest strode regally up the center aisle resting a large gold cross against one shoulder with two doting assistants—a girl and a boy—on either side of him carrying candles. After the cross and candles were placed on the altar, he faced the parish, glanced up at the balcony, and cued the choir to begin. They sang "Silent Night" in German so beautifully I was certain that angels had come down to hear. The priest then performed the mass in five different languages: German, Swiss-German, Italian, French, and English. He spoke extemporaneously repeating passages in the language he thought would best fit each one. He wasn't a typical Roman Catholic Priest; he wasn't following dogma, but instead listening to his heart. When he concluded, the parishioners were so enjoying the mass they were reluctant to leave. The service had elevated everyone, melding us into a family. The parents and children who had shared their pew hugged me and wished me a Happy Christmas. I felt so connected with them, it was difficult to say goodbye.

As we filed out the priest was standing outside on the front steps blessing each person. I thanked him for the celebration of Christmas that, for me, turned out to be much more than a mass. It felt more like an outpouring of love from the hearts of fifty-or-so divine souls. When our eyes met, if only for an instant, I knew that we both saw the Unbounded in the other.

I realized that what I knew as "Pure Consciousness," he saw as "Heaven." The two were the same.

Meditating with the Eyes Open

These glimpses of Pure Consciousness blossomed into further unexpected and joyful revelations. One bright morning, I stepped out onto my balcony to meditate just as the first rays of sun were illuminating the mountain tops and warming the air. I wrapped myself in my grey wool blanket and stuffed a feather pillow between my back and the wall. I spent a few minutes scanning the always incredible view in front of my eyes, but when I closed them to meditate, they immediately popped back open and felt as if they were going to stay that way.

I am sure the view made it happen.

I was fascinated by the golden sparkles of sunlight created by gusts of wind blowing across the surface of the lake. Then the sparkles joined, becoming a flat sheet of transparent gold that separated from the surface. The scene was ethereal and beautiful beyond belief. I attempted to close my eyes several times to no avail. They always flicked open, thirsting to take in the view. What was in front of me was too celestial, too perfect to be missed. It felt so right that there was nothing to do but allow it to happen. How could I not, with such exquisite beauty making itself known?

I realized that I was being shown something. This subtle field had always existed just beneath the surface and only needed to be accessed. It was there in meditation but also, it had been right in front of my eyes, and I had been looking past it.

Then the view gained a feeling of unreality. The more I relaxed, the flatter it became, as if the mountains, the sky, the clouds and their shadows on the surface of the lake, were projected onto a movie screen—yes, I remembered, Maharishi's movie screen in his talk at Humboldt. The more I relaxed, the more real the picture appeared until it was completely connected to me. And, then I realized I was creating the entire scene. *It was a projection of my mind and I was the projector.*

I could see the young man in the audience at Humboldt, in his brown jacket, standing at the mic asking the question, "Maharishi, I heard you say that on the path to realization, a man must experience himself as separate from the world, as witness to it."

I could hear Maharishi's answer as if there were no time existing between then and now.

"When the perception is individual, the awareness is overtaken by the object, and when the see-er cannot maintain himself and his awareness is overtaken, then Pure Awareness is not available. Like the white color of the cinema screen is not available, it is the picture that dominates and the real nature of the screen is not available."

His voice was as clear as if he was speaking in the present. "At the cost of the nature of the screen, the cinema is enjoyed" he said. "The perceptions of the world, the infinite perceptions, are all enjoyed at the cost of the real nature of the enjoyer."

And I could never forget his final words, spoken now as he did then, "The enjoyer himself is—we use the word, *bound*."

And yet, and yet… it came to me that I was *not* bound. Instead, I was all of what I was seeing. All of it. I realized that I hadn't lost the screen. The movie was playing on the screen that was me.

All This is That. And, I too, am That.

Then there was complete bliss. I was the bliss of being Consciousness itself. It was not really me because I was looking back at Tony sitting on the balcony of this hotel overlooking Lake Lucerne in Switzerland. The Tony on the balcony was just a body. A body with a mind trapped inside. But I was not him. I was no longer Tony. I was just bliss. I leaned back against the hard cement wall and felt a back and a body that were no longer mine.

Finally, these realizations exhausted me and my eyelids became heavy. I could no longer keep my eyes open and dozed off. I woke up in my old state of being, but the residue of what happened remained. In the coming days when I tried to revisit the experience, I couldn't. I consoled myself that I had accessed a new and finer level of reality, and even though I couldn't get it back, at least I knew it existed. Once again when I sat to meditate, I closed my eyes. My eyelids closed like curtain shades and I would be back in the silence, but now with the knowledge that infinite Consciousness also existed with open eyes. I knew that Consciousness could not be contained, it was everywhere, in everything, and I was it.

Maharishi often said that we are not individual, we are cosmic.

Now, I knew it was true.

A Visit from the Family

Living in the rarified atmosphere of Seelisberg, within Maharishi's darshan, my identity as Tony Anthony, who grew up in suburban Connecticut receded to the background.

But when I heard from my mother that she and my father were planning to visit, I was excited—even more so because my sister Pati was coming along. She and I hadn't spent much time together growing up. We went to different schools, different summer camps, and had our own sets of friends, so I was especially pleased to be able to connect with her. I booked them rooms in the tiny Hotel Loewen guesthouse next to the Waldhaus, where the hotel's gregarious innkeeper regaled them with tall tales about Switzerland. It turned out to be a perfect choice.

I never thought about the culture shock my family might experience by being in Maharishi's world for the first time. Since

I was just a humble worker-bee, and no one special in the hierarchy, I didn't expect Maharishi to acknowledge their presence, but I was wrong. At the first meeting they attended, Maharishi reserved seats for them in the front row of the hall, a place usually saved for honored guests. My mother awaited his arrival standing at the foot of his dais with a bouquet in her arms. Maharishi approached her immediately upon entering the hall and received the flowers with appreciation meant only for her. Whatever he said to her—which she never revealed—melted her heart. She returned to her seat beside me with her eyes sparkling and whispered in my ear, "I'm in love."

When the meeting began and Vesey Crichton, master of ceremonies, introduced my father as "Al Anthony, the king of advertising," I watched his ego expand. I was certain that Maharishi dictated those exact words to Vesey because they described perfectly how my father thought of himself. By the end of the evening assembly, my parents and my sister were visibly overwhelmed. Maharishi's darshan had created a bit of overload. None of them could remember a word he'd said in his talk.

My parents invited me to join them on a road trip for a week. They planned to drive first to Innsbruck, Austria where my father had an appointment to pitch a product idea to Helmut Swarovski, the head of the Swarovski Crystal empire, and then on to Venice. I told Maharishi about the invitation, he gave me his blessing and urged me to enjoy my family. He was happy, he said, that my family had come to Seelisberg.

We departed in the morning. Before we aimed for Austria we stopped in Lucerne where my father gave me the gift of a bank account that provided me with enough money for several future courses. This was totally unexpected, especially since my father, a self-made man who had grown up poor, believed that helping his kids with money was wrong. So, to say his gift stunned me is not an exaggeration. I attributed this sudden burst of generosity as a sign of Nature supporting me and to my father being in Maharishi's presence. But perhaps closer to the truth, he helped me because he saw the transformation I'd made from the deconstructed mess I'd been after Vietnam. I accepted the money willingly because it meant I could continue to follow the spiritual path I was on. It wasn't until later that I realized how big a deal the money was. It allowed me to attend every one of Maharishi's advanced courses during the coming years.

When my father announced that we would be staying in the finest hotel in Venice, the Gritti Palace, I was delighted I had brought my new Italian suit. Our holiday was wonderful. Driving south from Innsbruck, Austria to Italy we passed through some of the most beautiful countryside in Europe. Although I had spent years living in Switzerland, I had been so inwardly focused on my own spiritual development that I hadn't seen the totality of the beauty in the country and beyond. I gained a new pair of eyes in the relaxed atmosphere of being on vacation. Our conversations were mostly about what was going on with old family friends back in Connecticut. I was genuinely interested to know about all the relatives on both sides of the family. We didn't discuss what was happening with me in detail. For one thing, I knew the three of them were overwhelmed by the experience of being in Seelisberg and meeting Maharishi. Maharishi had that effect on almost everyone.

It wasn't until years later that Pati mentioned how strange the experience had been for her, being in the meeting hall with only men all dressed in suits and ties, all with pretty much identical haircuts and, for the most part, all pale and fairly emaciated. She told me she thought I had been captured by a strange cult. I replied, jokingly, that in a way I had and added, it was the most perfect cult I could imagine being captured by.

Pati and I shared a room in Venice and had the rare opportunity to catch up on each with long late-night conversations. Since we knew so little about each other, we were grateful for the chance to share personal aspects of our lives. Although Pati was curious about my life with Maharishi, I found it difficult to describe the intensity and joy of being around him. Whatever words I tried seemed like over-the-top platitudes, so I resorted to recounting my day-to-day life in Seelisberg. Pati told me she could see how far I had come from being a wounded veteran only a few years ago, and she admitted, that I now had "a certain glow."

Venice worked its magic on us. We enjoyed the sightseeing and the fantastic food so much that we extended the visit a few days. Pati and my parents were going to Rome next and invited me to join them. But even though I had only been away for just over a week, I was feeling homesick for Seelisberg and Maharishi. So, I boarded a train in Venice for Milan where I connected with another into Switzerland. At some point I realized I was on the same train that I watched from my balcony in the Kulm, the train that ran through the tunnel under Mt. Meru on the far side of the lake. I would get off in Brunnen and take the steamer to Treib that connected with the funicular, just as I had the first time I made the journey carrying my grandfather's suitcase.

I reserved a seat in a first-class compartment and ended up sharing it with an attractive woman in her thirties dressed like a hip Annie Oakley in a Western-style, suede-fringed jacket. She was a vivacious and talkative ex-patriot American named Liselotte Hohs, a painter and a longtime Venice resident. I was as curious about her life in Venice as she was about mine living in an ashram in the Swiss mountains. I relished her attitude, so dissimilar to the beliefs of the people around me. We talked non-stop to Lugano where she got off to attend the opening of an art show. Sometime later, I learned her popular naive-style paintings of Venice had made her a world-renowned artist.

After she departed, thoughts of her swam through my mind for hours rekindling my longing for a relationship with a woman. But as the train continued north through the breathtaking St. Gotthard Pass, I was happy once again for my simple ascetic life and the peace and joy it brought me. It was as if I had just put my toe in the water of the Relative and didn't really like the temperature. I considered that I might be becoming a devotee who would always want to stay under the safety of Maharishi's umbrella. But the deeper truth became evident when an image of Liselotte surfaced again.

I liked having a foot in both worlds.

Trouble in Paradise

While I was away, a traumatic event had pushed a somber cloud over Seelisberg. The heavy feeling in the air was palpable, yet no one mentioned it. Staff members went about their business as usual despite the obvious pall and no one would talk about it, even when I asked. Negative discussions were frowned upon and if anything adverse occurred, we weren't supposed to focus on it. Maharishi was fond of saying, "That which you put your attention on grows stronger," and everyone took his words to heart.

Over the next few days, the truth surfaced. Maharishi had invited a fellow Indian guru named Swami Muktananda to visit Seelisberg, and when he left, he enticed certain people to go with him. Several key staff members, including one of Maharishi's secretaries, had departed. Muktananda, who was reputed to be a master of siddhis, had presumably used them to lure the people away. The idea that a supposedly enlightened master would do such a thing was inconceivable to me and competition among enlightened masters was even more difficult to imagine. It was, however, undeniable that several top staff were gone, never to be seen again. I could understand when someone left in good conscience, but from what I learned, they seemed to have been victims of trickery. The rumor was that Muktananda had lured those who left with him with a promise of a quicker path to enlightenment.

I never heard Maharishi speak badly of Muktananda and I supposed that he understood the reasons for the departure. But, to me, the sudden breach of loyalty felt traitorous, especially for those so close to Maharishi. As I learned in the military, loyalty is one of the highest virtues. Without loyalty to fellow soldiers, wars cannot be won and without loyalty to Maharishi's cause, there was little chance of success. If we, who devoted our lives to bringing peace to the world, didn't remain loyal to our leader and honor his mission, how would the Movement succeed? To me, this incident brought up the bigger issue of the Movement's karma. I had always assumed that the World Government was in tune with the Laws of Nature that govern the cosmos. But if that were true, why did such negative events even happen? The only possibility I could think of was that Maharishi's Movement, as a whole, had a larger, collective karma that had to be worked out.

People close to Maharishi did leave from time to time, but most departed with dignity after a discussion with him. Fred Den Ouden, one of Maharishi's photographers, left with his blessings.

He was scrupulously honest and unsure about whether Maharishi was his true master. He shared his doubts with Maharishi and his desire to go to India to check out other teachers. Maharishi supported his quest and wished him well on his journey. After a year of searching ashrams in all parts of India, looking for a more enlightened guru, Fred returned to Seelisberg. He told me that none of the masters he met could hold a candle to Maharishi.

At this time, I had my own opportunity to reconsider my role in Maharishi's plan.

No matter where he was, Maharishi always sat on a deerskin. The signal that Maharishi was about to enter a meeting occurred when one of his secretaries entered carrying the deerskin. Thus, he was affectionately known as the "skin boy." I had moments when I thought about that position for myself. One of Maharishi's "skin boys" was a secretary who had departed with Muktananda. I was certain Maharishi was daring me to step up to the job. After one lecture in a meeting room where I had been sitting at his feet, Maharishi left the room when the skin boy was absent leaving the deerskin sitting on his couch. My heart pounded because I knew I was being handed this opportunity. The invitation was to become the one who entered every meeting hall first to set the deerskin on the couch. I had no doubt this was my chance to come forward. I'd had the same feeling when I'd realized that Maharishi wanted to hire me from the audience in Interlaken.

Using my shyness as an excuse for what was really a lack of confidence, I argued to myself that the role of skin boy was not for me. The duty of delivering Maharishi glasses of orange juice, with a napkin carefully folded over the top, as I had seen his skin boy do hundreds of times, seemed the ultimate way to be of service. But I also told myself that a position that required spending twenty-four hours each day, not only carrying the deerskin, but anticipating Maharishi's every desire by watching every subtle move he made, was more than I could handle.

I quickly talked myself out of it.

So, I left the hall without picking up the deerskin, breathing a sigh of relief tinted with sadness for a lost opportunity.

Whatever unspoken event had happened with the visiting guru was quickly forgotten and life on staff returned to normal. I went back to sharing the office with Eike and being a graphic designer, which felt right. But there was a subtle, yet undeniable sensation that something had shifted. There was an ominous feeling in the air, as if a storm was approaching.

Maharishi Weeds His Garden

*M*y feeling was prescient: A huge shift was about to take place. It began when Maharishi called a meeting in the new assembly hall which resembled the United States Senate chamber in Washington, now the official seat of the World Government for the Age of Enlightenment. Everyone who worked in Seelisberg was required to be at the meeting. The government consisted of the "108's," the one-hundred and eight young men who had the means to pay for the privilege of being around Maharishi. In essence, the 108's were, in Indian terms, the "Brahmans," the administrators, whereas the worker bees like myself were "Kshatriyas," the warriors who fought the battles.

As the event began, the feeling in the hall was somber. The meeting began with Maharishi on his couch scanning the room. On cue, Vesey Creighton stepped up to the podium and opened his folder as usual. He glanced down at the paper on top, looked up and announced that Maharishi wanted to assess everyone's position in The World Government. Vesey then read the name of the first person on what was obviously a list of names based on the seating plan, starting with the first person in the front row seated to Maharishi's right. The first two rows were the 108's.

Maharishi focused his full attention on the young man, as he did with each subsequent person. With some, he seemed to be satisfied with having them quickly explain their role—what their jobs were and what they were accomplishing. He would offer a "good—keep doing," nodded his approval and moved on. With others, the questions could be more pointed and personal. Sometimes he asked the kinds of questions he did in my job interview in the dark. Regardless of what he asked, he appeared to be taking a deep look inside each of us—perhaps to determine our usefulness in his plan.

Maharishi paused and turned irritated when he came to a fellow in the first row, a 108, and wasted no time in telling him he was no longer needed. He didn't leave it at that; he told him to leave Seelisberg immediately. There was a shocked silence in the hall. I wondered what Maharishi knew about him that I didn't. Whatever it was, the fellow seemed to know, and he stood up and walked out of the hall.

The inquisition went on for hours. I was nervous about what questions might be asked of me. But, hearing my name read, Maharishi smiled. I told him I was a designer, which he already knew. He said, "Yes, yes, you do good things." So that was that, and he went on to the next person.

Hours later, when he had finished reviewing everyone in the hall, he told us with a satisfied look on his face, how important we were to him. He said there was no need to be jealous of those taking the advanced courses then occurring all around us—as if we felt they were privy to some special knowledge. He assured us that our opportunity would come soon and said that we had everything we needed at the moment. In case we doubted our position in Maharishi's cosmos, he told us, "One glimpse of my dhoti is worth a lifetime of courses."

The Failure of America

At this time, I felt that I had reached the pinnacle of my position as one of Maharishi's designers. My creativity informed my design work and I could be proud of what I had accomplished. Even more important, I managed each project without the help of my ego. I was just me doing my job. I was reminded of my experience in the military where nothing is done for the self, but for a higher good. I felt like a consummate soldier in Maharishi's army.

However, the one constant in the Relative world is *change*. I should have known that. We were in a state of perpetual expectation, given that Maharishi was carrying us toward enlightenment at rocket speed. But the next change was as unexpected as it was momentous. It was a purge, a banishment on two levels. On the practical level, the expulsion affected just those of us around Maharishi. Since The World Government for the Age of Enlightenment governed on the level of consciousness, and since each of us in Seelisberg represented a nationality, the coming purge happened simultaneously with the staff as well as on a global scale.

International Staff was mostly a mixture of American, British, German, and Scandinavian. For some reason, although I was an American, Maharishi never considered me one. This may, or may not have been, the reason that I was an unacknowledged observer when Maharishi told the American leadership that they were no longer among his chosen. I was a witness to the event that would result in the exiling of the Americans from Seelisberg.

This is how it happened. An English friend, Paul Levy, who had the enviable job of caretaking Maharishi's apartment, invited me to join him one morning as he was heading in to clean up. The invitation came completely out of the blue—a certain hint that unknowingly Paul was serving as a messenger for a higher purpose. While Paul went about replacing flowers in vases and otherwise straightening up in the sitting room, I took a seat and thumbed through a book of photographs taken by Linda McCartney, Paul McCartney's wife. On the front piece was a hand-written note to Maharishi saying how much she and Paul loved and appreciated him.

The door was open to the adjoining room, Maharishi's bedroom. We could hear Maharishi loud and clear, talking on the speakerphone. I realized that he was talking to Jerry Jarvis and I immediately felt a sadness in my heart hearing the disappointed tone in Maharishi's voice. He was expressing his dissatisfaction with the United States.

On one hand, I wondered if I should be listening to a conversation that was none of my business yet, on the other hand, I knew I was there for a reason. In other words, I was supposed to hear what Maharishi was saying. Having been around Maharishi for years now, I knew that everything happened for a reason, even though at the time, my mind struggled to understand. It was not unusual for full understanding to come years later.

In this case, Jerry was the national leader of Maharishi's movement for the United States. I was an American and maybe that was reason enough. Everything that happened in Seelisberg couldn't be understood by the mind. Things happened on the level of Pure Consciousness—Pure Being—and could not be understood on the level of the mind.

This may be impossible to understand, but that's exactly the point.

I can't pretend to comprehend the deeper meaning of the conversation. Essentially, Maharishi told Jerry he had lost faith in America, the country he believed would enlighten the world. America had let him down. My heart was heavy when I heard this. I supposed that as an American, I too, had let him down. I couldn't imagine how Jerry must have felt. It was so difficult to listen to what Maharishi was saying that I wanted to cover my ears.

I felt so badly afterwards that I never told anyone—not even Eike—about what I heard. I couldn't imagine anyone more devoted to Maharishi than Jerry. Beginning on the day I was initiated, when I eavesdropped on the conversation he was having with my initiator, Kenny Edwards, Jerry served as an example of what it meant to devote one's life to the Master. He lived and breathed Maharishi's message and carried the TM organization in the United States forward for decades.

I was beginning to believe that much of what happened in Maharishi's Movement was dependent upon forces larger and much more powerful than met the eye. That being the case, Jerry, as the figurehead, was acting a role, and as such, he was more of a symbolic figure rather than a personal one. So, there was nothing personal about his demotion. What happened in the United States was a result of the collective consciousness of all the citizens, not just one. In the days to follow Maharishi talked openly about being let down by America. And then he acted on it. Again, in a meeting that shocked us all, he announced that all Americans should leave the Capital immediately.

One of Maharishi's junior secretaries, a diminutive fellow from Canada, had taken it upon himself to compile a list of all the names of all the Americans on staff, including mine. I heard that this overly officious fellow would bring the list to Maharishi's attention daily, in private meetings that excluded Americans. Someone who had been there told me that whenever Maharishi heard my name he would always reply, "Tony's not American—he went to the same school as Lawrence," the senior designer. I was spared for weeks until the zealous Canadian was insistent enough to convince Maharishi of my actual nationality. When Maharishi asked to meet with me, I knew why: It was my time. Maharishi, despite his initial reluctance, finally admitted the inescapable reality of my nationality.

It warmed my heart to know that he had kept me close for as long as he had.

I was called to meet with him in a small room that may have been the same one where I had my original job interview in the dark. This time, with the lights on, I could see Maharishi's face clearly. His expression was neutral and dispassionate, as if the decision for me to leave wasn't his, but an inevitability. Overhearing Maharishi's phone call with Jerry helped me understand that my dismissal wasn't personal.

But he wasn't firing me. Instead, I was being relocated to Livingston Manor in upstate New York and given the responsibility of opening a printing press like the one in Rheinweiler. I was going out into the world to do battle at "the front." Still, I would no longer be under Maharishi's protective umbrella. No longer in the presence of the Master I was so close to. My composure cracked with the impending pain of separation.

But then, I surprised myself.

Conquering the Catskills

When I departed Seelisberg the next day, I didn't feel I was leaving Maharishi, for he would always be with me. I felt sad leaving my close friends but my truest emotion was that of *relief*. Life was going to become less intense and far less demanding. As much as I loved being around Maharishi, the opposite was also true—I relished the freedom of being on my own. I took the steamer across to Brunnen to catch the train to Zurich, a trip I had made dozens of times to the art store. I spent a happy day in Zurich exploring the Old Town. I watched an art film made by Picasso's mistress and then had lunch at a Mövenpick restaurant before heading to the airport for my flight to New York. In Zurich, I felt like I was dipping my toe in the Relative World.

I was—and liking it.

Landing in America was yet more relief. For one thing, after years on foreign soil, I was returning to my own country. And, as blissful as life in Seelisberg could be, there was always an anxious undertone of trying to be as perfect as possible. Maharishi was the supreme taskmaster and as loving as he was, we felt his eyes on everything we did. This is not a negative, but the way a Master must behave to bring his disciples along. Now leaving Seelisberg behind, I felt a real sense of freedom. To compare it with the Army, leaving Switzerland was like being transferred from the field of combat to the safety of the rear where things are less dangerous and far less intense. After spending so much time evolving at rocket speed, I was quite comfortable with slowing down.

The driver from Livingston Manor who picked me up at the airport set a calm and relaxing tone for this last part of my journey. Even the old brown Chrysler station wagon he was driving foretold that an easier life lay ahead. Warm and friendly, and soft-spoken behind the wheel, he allowed the heavy vehicle to lumber along easily on the two-and-a-half-hour drive. We rode north from New York City through the Catskill Mountains, the former home of hotels like the Concord and Grossinger's, and a string of resorts, now in disrepair, that had catered to Jewish families in the summer. Passing the town of Liberty, at the crossroads of the Catskill Mountains and the Hudson Valley region, we drove along the Beaver Kill, a famous trout fishing river. Signs advertised bait-and-tackle stores, guns-and-ammo shops, fishing camps, and nothing much more—all around us was only wilderness.

Exiting the highway, we passed through the town of

Livingston Manor in about thirty seconds. There was a post office, two bars, an IGA grocery store, and some boarded-up storefronts. We climbed a hill for a few miles until turning onto a one-lane road marked by a sign with an arrow pointing to Lake Shandelee. Finally, we drove through two crumbling stone pillars and entered a driveway to a conglomeration of white stucco buildings. Once known as The Waldemere, the place had been a resort on 460 acres with a nine-hole golf course, over 200 rooms and a ten-acre lake. On the surface, this was a 1950's playground that had seen better days. Although the property had belonged to Maharishi for less than a year, the atmosphere had the uncommon but familiar feeling of deep silence that emanates from any group of Transcendental Meditators.

It felt like home. I felt like I had arrived at a Capital of the Age of Enlightenment.

Within a few days, I was acclimated and happy to reconnect with Duke Gibbs, "Flash" Pflaumer and Michael "Rio" Ritter from Santa Barbara. Together we claimed a corner table in the dining hall for ourselves where we joked about everything except our important mission. Maharishi wanted Livingston Manor to be a vital production hub for the Movement, second only to Seelisberg for the production of films, videos, and printed course materials. Most of these materials were for Maharishi International University, founded in Santa Barbara, now in Fairfield, Iowa.

Although the Capital was far from the center of Maharishi's universe, each department head received regular instructions from Seelisberg through the overseer, Bill Deknatel. Because we were our own bosses and were given a level of trust, we took our assignments seriously and aimed for excellence. Just like in Seelisberg, our missions were often challenging with unreasonable deadlines, as if to prove again and again that anything was possible. While I was setting up the graphics department and helping to start the press operations, the video guys were creating a broadcast level TV studio, called World Plan Television, that was being outfitted with the best cameras, a state-of-the-art control room, and an editing facility. MIU Press, as my project was named, purchased a five-color Heidelberg printing press from Germany which we set up in the basement of the dining room. As always in the miracle of the Movement, all the necessary pressmen and pre-press people, as well as a team of talented graphic artists and designers, manifested as needed.

Being at the Capital was stress-free. Everyone kept to the daily meditation routine followed by the siddhis and flying sessions. The isolated location, surrounded by nature, added to the serenity. The golf course was overgrown from lack of use, but Lake Shandelee became an after-dinner gathering place. A fleet of rowboats leftover from the resort made for blissful evenings floating on the lake. I was often joined by a friend, Martha Batorski, one of three sisters I nicknamed "The Flying Batorski Sisters." Martha's younger sister, Elizabeth, worked with me in the graphics department and I was also close to the youngest, Josie. Martha sat in the back of the boat facing me while I rowed us around the lake. We formed a close platonic relationship while discussing the mysterious journey of being on a spiritual path. It was a great joy to be in the company of women my age.

Every few weeks a new wave of TM meditators and teachers

showed up for advanced courses. On one such wave, I was immediately smitten by a tall and elegant young woman named Linda Wagoner. Seeing her gave me hope that there was, indeed, a woman meant for me. Unfortunately, with years of celibacy and lack of experience with the opposite sex, I was too shy to make contact and made her into an untouchable goddess. If I passed her in the hallway, I turned away for fear my blushing face would reveal my desire. Nonetheless, I was determined to express my secret love so, on a trip to New York City, I bought her a beautiful silk scarf at Tiffany's. Too frightened to present it to her in person, I left it for her as an anonymous gift at the front desk.

A day later I saw her wearing the scarf, such a pleasure in itself, that I let go of the idea of approaching her.

A Heart Full of Love

The freedom and spaciousness of Livingston Manor allowed my heart to soften and nurtured my platonic love for the Flying Batorski Sisters, and even fostered my sweet crush on Linda Wagoner. Whatever the cause, I found my heart expanding.

The design department, situated in the basement, bustled all day, but was quiet at night. It was the perfect place to sit silently at a typewriter and express the love I was feeling. I felt an undeniable expansion in my heart for Maharishi who had taught me so much after finding me destitute. I had no doubt he saved my life.

I sat at the typewriter night after night for weeks and wrote hundreds of poems.

These are a few:

Maharishi, please accept these words.

These poems are my voice—

that which I could not say for shyness

in your Holy Presence

I hope to sing to you here.

≈

My mind spins

in its love for you.

My heart cries out,

Oh, Lord, wherever you go

I ask, please take me with you.

≈

Glory are your white robes.

Glory is your Divine Stature.

Glory is your loving face.

≈

The sky fills with lotus flowers

because my heart is blossoming

with love and hope

and fullness of life.

≈

Maharishi, I love thee

I love thee with all my heart.

≈

I look and look

and cannot fathom you,

you who have given me life.

How can I ever repay thee?

My One Beloved Master

No star shines as bright.

A Door that Couldn't be Closed

The TM Movement was turning the Catskill Mountains into a spiritual haven. Maharishi purchased another former resort hotel, The Windsor, in South Fallsburg, about twenty minutes away. But other spiritual disciplines were part of the transformation, too. A Buddhist sect was beginning construction on a temple in nearby Roscoe, New York.

One morning, I was called into Bill Deknatel's office for a message fresh from Seelisberg.

"Maharishi wants to make South Fallsburg another Capital of the Age of Enlightenment. He wants an apartment for himself, a home away from home." Bill smiled knowingly and told me, "Maharishi said, 'Tony will design the capital.'"

I left Bill's office feeling joyous and filled with confidence with the knowledge that Maharishi had put his trust in me. The graphics department was up and running, staffed with capable people like Jimmy Collins, Tobi Fineblum and Elizabeth Batorski who would keep things moving, while I tackled this exciting new project.

I drove the lumbering brown Chrysler to see the old Windsor Hotel. The buildings had been built decades earlier but were well kept. The hotel was a rambling two-story affair with white clapboard siding set back from a sleepy country road, more reminiscent of an elegant New England inn than a Borscht Belt resort. It reminded me of New Hampton, New Hampshire where I went to prep school. I was immediately comfortable with transforming the place into a Capital of the Age of Enlightenment, confident that I had the knowledge and skill to do it. I had been trained well in Seelisberg.

I knew most-definitely that the first element should be an elegant wooden sign that would begin the transformation. I had "The Capital of the Age of Enlightenment" hand-painted in Times Roman letters in gold against a white background within, of course, a gold border. This was the timeless style created by Maharishi and the designers in Seelisberg that came before me and would continue with those who followed after. It was no surprise that the sign manifested effortlessly and was ceremoniously unveiled only a few days later at the driveway entrance. Elegant and welcoming, it had the amazing transformative effect that I knew it would.

My next priority was to turn a wing of the new Capital into an elegant suite of rooms. Having witnessed the construction of his apartment in Seelisberg, I visualized the suite with silk wallpaper covering the walls, dark blue carpets on the floors, and with a few artful furnishings for Maharishi and his guests. Thanks to Paul Levy, I knew details of Maharishi's preferences right down to the Pears Soap for the bathroom and Bloomingdale's finest white cotton bath towels. I was excited—brimming with joy, was more like it—with the project. I was given an American Express card to fund my shopping trips to New York. Of course, I was keenly aware that I was spending Movement money, so I booked a room at the moderately priced Hilton in midtown Manhattan, convenient to everything. Each day after morning meditation, I took the Fifth Avenue bus downtown to the D & D Building (Decoration and Design) which had floors of showrooms for all the top interior design companies. I went from showroom to showroom filled with the joy of creating a beautiful and comfortable apartment for my beloved Maharishi.

The project, as with any undertaking for Maharishi, revealed subtler levels as it unfolded. On the most basic level, I was designing a suite of rooms. But, beneath that was what the assignment was teaching me. This was no different than every other project I had worked on for Maharishi, there was a lesson to be learned. Subconsciously, I realized how far I had come from the day I showed up at Humboldt for my first course. I never imagined in a million years—and I do mean a million—that I would become an excellent designer, something that would be invaluable to supporting my family in the future. But more than just the design skills—understanding shapes and their special relationships, color theory, and the intricate processes of producing visual printed materials, the most important thing I had acquired was confidence. Because I knew the design world from top to bottom, I projected this assurance to others, sometimes to my astonishment. This is not an ego thing, just a revelation that I owned my skills.

And for this, I was eternally grateful.

Maharishi had not only saved me from the downward spiral I was in years earlier, but he gave me a useful trade. There was a moment during one of my morning meditations at the Hilton, where I saw myself not far from where I was sitting as a successful graphic designer. Although I can't honestly say that I saw into the future, only a few years would pass before I would be living in a garden apartment on the upper West Side making more money than I ever dreamed possible.

I selected fine silk wallpaper from Brunschwig & Fils in subtle shades of yellow and gold for his sitting room and bedroom. I purchased simple, yet elegant, shell-design gold faucets from Sherle Wagner, and fabric to upholster the couch and chairs from Clarence House. The American Express Card I had been given seemed to have no limits. When a project was for Maharishi personally, everything was unbounded.

Back in South Fallsburg, Movement volunteers were bringing things together effortlessly. For some jobs like paper hanging that required expertise, we readily found local tradespeople who were now out of work but who long ago, had worked at the old, now defunct, resorts: painters, paper-hangers, plumbers, carpet installers. Given the demise of those resorts, they were thrilled to find work with us and as excited as we were to see the Windsor being rehabilitated. There was none of the animosity we ran into with the Swiss craftspeople who had a hard time accepting work from the "Ru's." The citizens of the Catskills were just the opposite; they were happy we were there. I thought to myself that we were transforming the area one resort at a time, revitalizing it with an influx of meditators and Siddhas. The bottom line was, we were establishing Pure Consciousness in the Catskills.

While some were astounded at how easily Maharishi's suite emerged in a regal style befitting a great Master for all time, I felt the joy of knowing that I was merely the facilitator for the Grand Designer Herself, Mother Nature. I could take no credit for any of it; I was simply the witness to the action and the eventual accomplishment.

As we were nearing completion, word came that Maharishi was on his way to New York City and wanted to visit the new Capital. His timing was perfect, of course, and he arrived on the day our work was done. The carpets were laid, the wallpaper was up, the paint was dry, the towels were hung and the soap was in the soap dishes. The last thing on my list was plugging in seven new white telephones that had arrived that morning.

The moment I had finished installing the last phone in the sitting room, word came that Maharishi had arrived at the front door of the Capital and was heading to the suite. I hurried, hoping to vacate the premises before his arrival. I did a final check of each phone and raced out the door where I saw Maharishi just then rounding the corner at the far end of the hallway. I stopped, frozen in the doorway, and put my hands together in the traditional greeting. He looked up at me from far down the hall. My heart opened the way it had the first time I saw him. And a powerful rush of energy shot up my spine.

I was overwhelmed as he walked toward me, followed by Nandkishore and the usual retinue of secretaries and dignitaries. I hardly noticed who they were as he approached and stopped an arm's length in front of me. He said, "I've heard you've been doing good things," and my heart melted.

The words didn't matter, they could have been any words. It was that deep communication between an unbounded being that finds the same unbounded place existing in another. Pure Consciousness meeting Pure Consciousness. I searched for some words, but found none. Words felt useless for what I needed to express. What needed to pass between us—from the devotee to the Master and from the Master to the devotee—traveled from heart to heart where a deeper sense of understanding was involved. The transmission bypassed the mind.

Maharishi showed none of the disappointment about America that he had expressed in Seelisberg. Instead, he was warm and friendly. I followed him into the apartment where Nandkishore lay his deerskin on a couch in the sitting room. Maharishi sat and scanned the room and his smile said everything. I put my palms together again, said, "Jai Guru Dev," and started to leave. As I stepped into the hall, I grabbed the doorknob to close the door. But something made me stop and look back at Maharishi sitting on the couch. I let go of the knob, leaving the door open. It didn't feel right to have a closed-door between my Master and me.

The next day I found Nandkishore and told him I wanted to speak with Maharishi. He smiled at me from behind his glasses and shiny black beard without asking why, perhaps already knowing. I followed him into the sitting room where Maharishi was talking on the phone looking very much at home.

When he finished his conversation, I told him I had a strong desire to marry and have a family.

Maharishi smiled impishly. He told me something unexpected. "Then you should move to MIU."

I had never considered this as an option. After all, I had already pictured myself living in New York as a successful art director. Unanticipated thoughts filled my head: MIU was co-ed; there were women there. Maybe I would find a mate. Maybe Maharishi knew something I didn't. It was a short conversation that seemed to form a plan set in stone. As I turned to go, Maharishi looked at Nandkishore, who handed me what turned out to be a priceless gift—a slip of paper with Maharishi's phone number on it.

Maharishi said, "You can call me anytime."

And I was out in the world.

A Brief Stop at MIU

The world I had hoped for was not Maharishi International University. I arrived in the soggy midwestern heat in Fairfield, Iowa, in my newly purchased used red and white Volkswagen bus, a near duplicate of the one Gloria and I drove to Humboldt in eight years earlier. Even though the administration knew Maharishi had sent me, I couldn't find a path into the college's life. I didn't have a college degree, so I couldn't teach. The graphics department was operating just fine, so my talent as a designer was unnecessary. So, the question became, "What am I doing here?" I was a fish out of water.

Even my surroundings were unsettling. At the time, the place was more of a conglomeration of mismatched buildings than a campus. There was an odd group of two-story octagonal brick structures called pods that looked like a spacecraft from another galaxy. Only one building, covered with ivy, looked anything like it belonged to a university. Because there was no central quad, it was difficult to distinguish the borders between the university and the town. The town of Fairfield was a bland architectural desert on its own with boring local shops facing a barely landscaped square. The fact that I didn't want to be there made the place all the more depressing.

To make matters worse, I was assigned a room in a pod reserved for male faculty located on a far edge of the campus bordering a cornfield. The view from my window was flat farmland devoid of hills, barren of trees. My housemates were the same professors I had designed graphics for in Santa Barbara at the very beginning of my time with Maharishi, yet they barely welcomed me. I felt as if I had been sentenced to live with them. And finally, it was near the end of the school year and the students would be leaving, so there wasn't much of a chance to meet my future wife.

The silver lining was that my experience in Fairfield was painful enough to lead me to act. I knew it was pointless for me to try to fit in—it just wasn't my place. Since there was no need to prolong the pain, I had to consider a final exit. And I knew the only way out was for me to tell Maharishi how I felt.

As it happened, graduation day for the university was also to be my graduation from the Movement.

On that day, the student body was gathered in the auditorium for Maharishi's commencement address via satellite. I took a seat in the back row. Although I had come a long way and was no longer the ex-soldier who imagined gunning down the audience,

I felt I had come full circle. My reasons were different, but sitting in the back row was where I belonged. Hours passed while Maharishi kept the audience waiting, which came as no surprise to me. A different university official would appear on stage every so often to deliver an update with the same message each time: "Maharishi will speak to us soon."

I smiled inwardly knowing the Master would likely keep the students waiting in the auditorium all day, possibly even longer. I realized Maharishi was giving the graduating class a necessary lesson in patience. The students were given a lunch break and returned to their seats afterward, eagerly awaiting Maharishi who would talk to them by speakerphone. Two o'clock rolled around and he still hadn't called.

I had enough waiting. Waiting had given me the time to make up my mind. With no lingering doubt about leaving Fairfield, I stood up and left the hall. I walked into town in search of a phone booth and found one outside the Baskin-Robbins ice cream shop. I knew Maharishi had given me his phone number for just this moment. I dialed the number in Seelisberg, billing the call to my credit card, and waited, listening to the sounds of the electronic connections. Then came the high-pitched Swiss ring of Maharishi's phone followed miraculously by Nandkishore's voice. "Yes?"

"Nandkishore, this is Tony Anthony. I would like to speak with Maharishi."

"Yes, yes—he's right here."

While I was somewhat amazed that I had gotten through so easily, I heard Nandkishore say my name out loud. My heart pounded at the sound of Maharishi's voice over the speakerphone.

The intensity of having Maharishi's full attention made me get to the point quickly.

"Maharishi, this is Tony Anthony. I'm at MIU. I'm unhappy here and I want to leave." That was all I said and all I needed to say.

He asked me what I was planning to do. I told him my father had asked me to join him in his work.

Maharishi replied, "If the business is successful, then join your father. Go, and do good things." He paused a moment and said a few words that warmed my heart: "Come back whenever you like."

I thanked him, and that was that. I felt lighter, lifted by an amazing sense of relief. My eight-year tenure had just come to an end. I had resigned with dignity. Most importantly, I had left with the Master's blessing.

I bought myself an ice cream cone at Baskin-Robbins, stopped by the auditorium, stuck my head in the door and heard Maharishi addressing the students.

The next morning, I took off without saying a single goodbye. I was driving towards freedom and I didn't want to look back. It felt wonderful to be perched behind the wheel of a VW bus again steering into the adventure ahead.

Back in the World

*D*riving south from Iowa felt like coasting downhill from the Swiss Alps to the Florida seashore. I followed a map southeast towards my father's business in Sarasota with the idea of helping him create useful products for the home, which is what he did. I thought of it as doing good things. Spending time at my parent's beautiful home on the Gulf of Mexico seemed like another good thing. I was reconnecting with Planet Earth— walking along the beach on solid ground, taking breaks to swim in a turquoise sea.

Now I had the time and space to step back from the intense experiences of the past years, and maybe even sort them out. I thought some physical distance from Maharishi would help me see things clearly. I had no mixed feelings about leaving. Instead, I saw endless possibilities ahead. There was a whole new world in which I knew I could accomplish whatever I wanted. Driving through the South, I saw the world a simple place and I was confident I had gained the knowledge I needed to conquer it. I carried the zealousness instilled in me in Seelisberg knowing that anything was possible. For years, I had been on an adventure that took me deep within. Maharishi called it "the inward stroke," and now I was prepared for the outward stroke.

In the end, I didn't remain in Florida long. I wasn't satisfied working for my father; the business was his dream, not mine. My real goal was to conquer New York and after a few months, I moved there to take on the big city. To me, New York was the ultimate proving ground for graphic designers. The competition was stiff but the payoff was great. So, filled with the sense of unlimited potential that Maharishi had imbued in me—the belief I could do anything—I dove into finding work.

I received the Support of Nature Maharishi had promised; miracles unfolded one after another. With the help of an uncle, my first client became the United States Mission to the United Nations. The public relations director loved my work, amazingly enough, because all my samples contained pictures of Maharishi. It turned out the U.N. had its own Indian Guru and most of the employees of the mission were followers. Not only did I secure a job designing brochures, but within a few weeks, I was given the honor of designing the United Nations Day poster for that year. My career flourished. I gained recognition for the poster, which I had printed at the MIU Press in Livingston Manor. On a flight home after attending an advanced TM course, I sat next to the owner of a travel-accessories company who interviewed me for the job of creative director. By the time we landed, he had tentatively hired me. After a short trial period, I secured the job. Another miracle. Within a year of leaving the Movement, I was making enough money to afford a garden apartment in a brownstone on the Upper West Side of Manhattan.

But when I heard that Maharishi was giving a course in India on Vedic Science in India, I couldn't pass up the chance to be with him again and took a leave of absence from work.

I had always longed to go to India.

Last Stop, India

The Vedic Science Course for Siddhas and TM Teachers in India was to be held in a desert town called Noida, southeast of New Delhi. Maharishi had determined that this was the site of a famous battle described in The Bhagavad Gita, one of the major holy scriptures of Hinduism. It is where the warrior Arjuna receives life lessons from Lord Krishna. Maharishi's translation and commentary of the epic was a bestseller that had been my bedtime reading for years. It was the best guidebook for a spiritual life I had ever encountered for anyone whose goal was to attain enlightenment in this lifetime. It is safe to say that this was a common goal among Maharishi's followers. We were all searching for self-realization.

Maharishi's words from Chapter Five, Verse 24 of the Bhagavad Gita are, "He whose happiness is within, whose contentment is within, whose light is all within, that yogi, being one with Brahman, attains eternal freedom in Divine Consciousness." Here he writes of a state beyond Cosmic and Unity Consciousness called Brahman. It seemed to me that being in India with Maharishi held open the door to Cosmic Consciousness. This meant crossing the threshold to the freedom from bondage of self and looking back through the doorway at the illusory world of the Relative

Although I had been away from the Movement for more than a year, the thought of a course to study the Vedas with Maharishi was a magnet drawing me back to him. Having been on the outward stroke *integrating*, the thought of being in his presence for a deep dive into Being created waves of bliss. In addition to Maharishi's presence, the course application announced there would be 5,000 pandits performing Vedic recitations. Just to think all this would be taking place in India, the place he called the birthplace of spiritual knowledge, there was no way I wouldn't be part of it.

The moment I stepped off the plane in New Delhi I was in love with India. I felt totally comfortable in the throngs of people packed in long lines waiting to have their passports checked. The hall, filled with so many human beings, felt incredibly familiar to me. Interacting with Indians, I felt more like them than American, and I was certain I had spent one—or more likely *many*—lifetimes there. Intuitively, I understood, like an Indian would, the need to have my passport and visa stamped by three different immigrations agents, each time with much ceremony and dignity. India was exotic like Vietnam, only in a much more beautiful and "sattvic" (life-affirming) way. While Vietnam had steamy, dark energy, India was imbued with softness and light.

My trusted travel companion, my Grandfather's battered leather suitcase only made it as far as Paris, but I was so happy to be in India, I didn't mind at all. Somehow, this made perfect cosmic sense. The missing luggage gave me the excuse to buy some new clothes—Indian style shirts called kurtas that extend to the knees. Loose cotton pants with drawstrings completed my outfit and put a smile on my face. After all, I'd finally managed to arrive at the dress code I'd once believed was for "serious spiritual seekers." I laughed at the thought, but I still felt the joy of being Indian. I'd come home.

Maharishi's Indian staff greeted us with the news that 'Vedic City,' the tent encampment where we were to live, wasn't yet ready for us. After all, we were told, it was being built almost overnight to house 2,000 course participants as well as 5,000 pandits. In the meantime, we were booked into hotels, large and small, in all parts of New Delhi. My friend and now roommate, Jonathan Rosen, and I were driven by taxi to an address that turned out to be a pleasant B&B in the suburbs.

Although the course was officially set to begin on the night of Mahalakshmi, one of the holiest celebrations of the year in India, we were told we could attend a special puja the Vedic pandits were performing in honor of Lakshmi, the goddess of wealth and good fortune, on her birthday. Buses were sent to gather up all the course members for a two-hour ride to Noida. We left New Delhi at dusk with the sun setting in a deep orange red sky, heavy with smoke from cooking fires. Within minutes, we were driving through a rural landscape passing camels carrying heavy loads across a desert. By the time we reached Vedic City, it was pitch black. Stepping off the bus we faced a huge sea of white canvas tents topped with poles flying flags of every color. We could hear the faint sound of the pandits' chanting coming from somewhere far off. I was swept by the crowd down a dirt thoroughfare with bulbs strung on wires overhead lighting our way. We were drawn by the mystical sound of the chanting, growing louder as we walked, until we reached a gigantic tent where the chanting became overwhelming.

Indians in white dhotis greeted us at the entrance. Leaving our shoes outside, we stepped barefoot into another world, a creation of the powerful chanting of the 5000 pandits. Crossing the threshold was leaving solid earth and stepping into another, subtler realm. The light in the tent was softened by a haze of incense drifting from a stage at the far end. I was entering a universe I had never imagined, where powerful waves of sound permeated my body making it vibrate with a kind of celestial energy.

When my eyes began to adjust, rows-upon-rows of pandits emerged from the dark, seated on carpets facing a puja underway on the stage. More than a dozen holy men in dhotis of different colors sat cross-legged on the floor facing an image of the Goddess Lakshmi and a live saint resplendent in an orange robe. I recognized the golden throne he sat on, and the umbrella above him, from black and white photos of Guru Dev. Like Guru Dev, his forehead was painted with three horizontal lines, the sign of Shiva, the embodiment of Pure Consciousness. I assumed the saint on the stage must be the current Shankaracharya of Jyotir

Math, the northern seat of Shankara's knowledge. I knew that the first Shankaracharya of the north was Totakacharya.

At first, I couldn't find Maharishi. I was used to seeing him in the center of the stage. I searched carefully before I spotted him uncharacteristically seated on the floor facing the Shankaracharya. It was odd to see my Master in what seemed like a position of servitude, until I realized he was performing this act of humility out of devotion to his Master, Guru Dev. I imagined him sitting at Guru Dev's feet in the same way. I thought that for Maharishi, this Shankaracharya embodied Guru Dev. By this show of humility, he was also paying respect to the lineage of the great Masters of the Holy Tradition. Once again, Maharishi was setting an example for us all. And, once again, I was overcome with undying love.

I needed to get closer. There were no guards to stop me, so I made my way up a narrow aisle between the rows of pandits until I reached the stage. I found a space between two Indian devotees with a clear view of Maharishi. Standing there, the powerful chanting grew louder and the reverberations stronger. Maharishi and the holy men who flanked him on both sides were performing a puja while pandits delivered them offerings of fruits and flowers in baskets. Seated pandits circled flaming chalices of burning camphor and shining brass containers of sandalwood incense. At one point in the puja, two men brought forth a heavy basket of gold coins and, at Maharishi's direction, poured them onto a carpet at the feet of the Goddess Lakshmi.

Meanwhile, the pandits' voices grew louder inflating the giant tent with intensity. Suddenly, playing out right in front of my eyes, all the holy men on the stage including Maharishi, became characters taken from the pages of the Bhagavad Gita. This certainly didn't seem real in any earthly sense. On one hand, I was peering into some celestial level of existence and yet, on the other hand, simultaneously, whatever was happening in front of me was not really happening at all. It was a total contradiction. What I was seeing was incredibly captivating to my earthly senses and yet I knew it to be pure illusion. It was happening and not happening at the same time. It was the *Lila*, the Divine Mother's celestial play of creation,

My mind couldn't comprehend what my eyes were seeing. But by now, I knew that it was all taking place *beyond the mind.*

When the puja ended and the chanting suddenly stopped, the giant tent with all of us in it, sank into a deep, unmoving silence. My body was frozen in place, my eyes closed and I was enveloped in a most blissful samadhi. After a few minutes, I heard some movement on the stage, opened my eyes and saw the Shankaracharya making his way across the stage and down some steps with Maharishi and the others following.

The next day, dressed in my kurta, I explored the city by Tuk-tuk, the three-wheeled taxis with a passenger seat in back, driven by a man in front on an attached motor scooter. With the events of the last evening still playing in my head, even the smoke-laden air of New Delhi was blissful. At my request, the driver took me to a shop where I bought a set of colored markers in a metal box and a sketchbook. The ones I'd intended for India were somewhere in Paris. I was deliriously happy to once again possess the necessary tools for sketching, since my plan was to do a series of color drawings of my impressions of India.

The course began the next day. Our meetings with Maharishi were being held on the top floor of the *India Times* office building, a voluminous space donated by the publisher of the newspaper, a devotee of Maharishi. The entire floor of the building, a room large enough to hold the 2,000-and-more attendees, had been cleared of all furniture. The floor had been covered with foam mattresses fitted with sheets for the participants to sit on and use for meditation and the siddhis flying program. I arrived early for Maharishi's talk and found the room already packed with eager course participants. I looked for a place as far away from Maharishi as possible because I feared that if he spotted me, he'd put me to work and my course would be over. Maharishi's dais was positioned at one end of the room near the entrance. I found a spot in a remote corner behind one of the pillars that ran through the center of the room. I made myself comfortable leaning back against the pillar, and sank into meditation while waiting for Maharishi to arrive. When he did, a murmur of excitement went through the crowd and I took a peek around the pillar to get a quick glimpse before ducking back out of sight.

I placed my sketchbook on my lap ready to start drawing. As I was opening my new box of pens for the first time, I heard a tapping noise from the speaker on the pillar above my head. I recognized the familiar sound. Maharishi was testing his microphone. Then his voice followed. He complained, "They've left me no pens. How am I to write without pens?"

Maharishi's secretaries always set out a few colored pens and a stack of blank paper on the coffee table in front of him. I wondered how could they have forgotten? I heard Maharishi again. "These pencils—how can I write with these cheap pencils?"

As much as I wanted to deny it, in some inexplicable way, what was taking place involved me and my new box of pens. That was how things worked with Maharishi. Often, they couldn't be explained. But I knew I had to face the reality: Even though my pens and I were hidden from his view, he had tuned in on us. The jig was up. My box of pens was a goner, and so was I.

My course was over even before it began. My dream of a restful month rounding in India had been just a pipe dream. Resigned to my new fate, I closed the cover on my box of pens, picked up my pad and made my way through the crowd of seated meditators. As I approached a section in front of the dais reserved for special guests, I was held back by one of the German guards. I showed him my box of pens and then held them up for Maharishi to see. Maharishi nodded his approval and the guard let me pass. Maharishi gave me a pixyish smile when I stopped in front of him and opened the box to show him the pens. He smiled even wider when I set the box on his coffee table. As I turned to leave, he pointed a finger towards the floor and said, "stay." There was a place at his feet reserved for me. It was where I belonged.

The German guards took note, and I would not be held up for the remainder of the course—my place at the Master's feet was secure. I was back to being a designer—the only one here. Immediately after sitting down, Maharishi leaned forward, took a turquoise pen from the box and began sketching on a piece of paper. When he finished, he slowly slid the piece of the paper off the edge of the table. I caught it mid-air. Not surprisingly, he spoke the words he had written on the paper to the audience. This was "pure Maharishi," acting from the level of Brahman where everything is part of the divine flow that only he understands and we can only marvel at. He'd written the words both in Sanskrit and English. "He who is awake, the Richas seek him out." Then I got my instructions as he told both the audience and me simultaneously. "Soon we will have posters on all the walls. Tony will do it."

Hearing him say my name, what was left of my heart melted into pure bliss.

My experience working with Maharishi had always been that every project had two reasons for being. The first was to manifest the Master's desire and produce the actual project. The second reason was the underlying lesson. In this particular case, it was revealed in Maharishi's scribbles on the paper. *"He who is awake, the Richas seek him out."*

As I simultaneously both read and heard the words, they penetrated through my body into the core of my being. This particular message actually embodied all his teachings. Being *awake* meant first waking up to the reality of who we really are. In other words, become enlightened. Then and only then do we get the full support of Nature—because we are then acting in accord with Nature. It could be said that we are one and the same. *Richas* is a Sanskrit word meaning Laws of Nature. But it is imperative that enlightenment come first. As I've heard Maharishi say again and again, "Capture the fort and gain all the surrounding territory."

The profound beauty of Transcendental Meditation is that it takes us out of the mind, where we can experience Pure Consciousness, which is what we are. We are not the mind that doubts our true unbounded nature, we *are* our true unbounded Self.

As Maharishi went on talking about the Vedic Science Course, I sat at his feet feeling his silent stillness envelop me. I saw how simple enlightenment really is. It was so close, it had been staring me in the face all along. It's so simple that the mind can't grasp it and the eyes look right past it.

To manifest the Master's desire, I first had to learn to negotiate Old Delhi. *New* Delhi, India's capital, is an elegant cosmopolitan city built around wide tree-lined boulevards with government buildings designed by the British in Gothic style. In contrast, being in Old Delhi is descending into a third-world city with narrow streets packed with a wonderful mix of humanity, doing very human things, and sacred Brahman cows roaming the streets as they please. It is also where the typesetters, pre-press services and printing shops were. It felt great to be immersed in the city's divine chaos.

I introduced myself to Maharishi's Indian staff because they controlled the money and the services necessary to producing printed materials required cash. On each outing, I was supplied with a bag of Indian rupees always followed by a reminder to bargain Indian-style, which is to begin every negotiation by halving the asking price. Armed with that knowledge, negotiating became fun, and I found Indians easier to deal with than tough New Yorkers. After a few days, printed posters, with Maharishi's favorite gold borders, hung on all the walls of the hall.

After a few days of living in New Delhi, everyone moved to the tent compound in Noida, named Vedic City. This meant we commuted for more than an hour each way, to and from the *Times*

Building, for Maharishi's talks and rounding. As celestial as Vedic City had looked the first night during the Mahalakshmi puja, it appeared far different in the light of day. The lines of tents in the desert reminded me of a refugee camp in Vietnam. Both looked and smelled similar. The village was surrounded by a moat for sewage that was quickly overwhelmed by a population of 7,000 humans. In the intense desert heat, the resulting smell could be unbearable. While Indians might be used to such conditions, the Westerners weren't. I knew that on a spiritual level, there was a reason Maharishi had installed us there, but I had no idea what that might be. People began to fall sick with dysentery, which I had suffered from in Vietnam and didn't want to battle again. An old friend came to my rescue and offered to share a suite at the Ashok Hotel in New Delhi, which surely saved me from the scourge. The sick were tended to and were brought back to health in a makeshift clinic on the floor beneath the lecture hall in the Times building.

As the month-long course was coming to an end, Maharishi announced a two-week extension to further explore the Vedas. Without having to think about it, I took a taxi to the American Express office where they loaned me the money to cover the course fee. Those two weeks were totally blissful. My days were spent at the Master's feet without any further projects, which meant I could finally relax and enjoy the course. Between lectures, I spent time with friends walking and talking in the city park close to the *Times* building. The women on the course were stunning, wrapped in their colorful saris. They seemed to float across the grass while the men among us sat and chatted with Indians on park benches. In a month we'd all become Indians. At times, the scene in the park seemed so exquisitely beautiful, it reminded me of the play of life, the *Lila*. The figures, the flowers, the trees, seemed not to belong to this Earth. I was beginning to think that neither did I.

One day in the lecture hall, I smiled at the German guard as I passed on the way to my sacred space in front of Maharishi's table. I stood up when Maharishi came in, and I felt that, in passing, he was reminded of something. After he settled on the couch, he picked up a blue pen and began to sketch. From my vantage point, I couldn't see the paper. But when he finished drawing, he picked the paper off the table and folded it in half. He ran his index finger very precisely along the crease to make it a crisp fold. Then he opened it and drew a series of lines inside of what I now knew to be a brochure. The fold on a single sheet of paper was the clue that it would be a four-page booklet. He then closed it, turned it over and did a quick scribble.

I had been so laser-focused on watching him, that I hadn't heard a thing he'd been talking about. When I tuned in, I heard him say what a great honor it was to have the Shankaracharya's presence on Mahalakshmi to inaugurate the course. He talked about how the current Shankaracharya was our opportunity to connect with the great Masters of the Holy Tradition. When he said, "This was Guru Dev's seat," I felt a wave of love emanate from his heart. He went on to say, "It doesn't matter who the Shankaracharya is, it's what he represents that's important. He is our connection to all the great saints. Then he spoke in Sanskrit, reciting the names of the saints and I realized he was reciting the opening stanza of the puja. He continued until the last verse: "Brahmananda-Sarasvatim Guruvaram, Dhyayami Jyotir-Mayam."

When he finished, I watched his hand very slowly push the paper to the edge of the table. He stopped it there, which made me look up at his face. It seemed that Maharishi was no longer occupying his body, that something other—Pure Consciousness, I was sure—was there.

Then the paper slipped off the edge of the table and I caught it. As I studied it, Maharishi was focused in on me. "Put the Shankaracharya on the cover. Inside, one of the pandits will write some verses honoring him." Maharishi smiled. "On the back, you see India enlightening the world." I turned the paper over and saw that he'd drawn a map of the world with India in the center.

Before he went back to addressing the audience, he finished my instructions with, "You will make it beautiful." It was strange, but for an instant, it sounded as if he were talking to himself, that I was not even there, which actually was my experience.

When I tried to stand up to go, I found myself unable to move. I was frozen in space and time, as if there *were* no space nor time. I could find no being that I could call "me." And, there was no separate Being that was Maharishi. There was just one Being which made up all existence. Whomever I was, saw that the Cosmic Being was what existence actually was, which made me realize how ignorant it is to think of ourselves as individuals. That, in itself, is the cause of all heartbreak and sorrow. Embracing what we really are, we know that we are nothing but Consciousness itself, infinite, unbounded and cosmic.

When I finally stood, I wondered if my legs would support me. I felt myself coming back into my earthly body with all its weight and sensations. It took a few moments before I was able to walk. The German guard grinned at me broadly when I passed, as if I was his friend.

I stopped at the entrance door and glanced back. Looking around the room, I was seeing not from the perspective of a person named Tony, no separation between myself and others existed. We were one. My Being encompassed everything in the room—all the people, all the posters on the walls, all the courses, all the yearning for spiritual transcendence.

I was Cosmic and I knew I had really never been anything else.

A Joy-Filled Amazement

I booked a window seat for the first leg of my trip home, a nine-hour flight from Delhi to Paris, so I could rest my head on a pillow stuffed into the space between the seatback and the window. As I relaxed with deep breathing, somewhere over Afghanistan, I became mesmerized by an army of puffy white clouds lined up across the horizon. Watching them glide by ever so slowly, I drifted into the gap and found my Self somewhere between waking and dreaming.

Floating through my mind were thoughts of the night in Seelisberg when Maharishi inaugurated the Dawn of the Age of Enlightenment. There I was, all decked out in my new Italian suit, feeling like I had been promoted to captain. I even had a gold pin on my lapel with a sunrise and the words *Founding Governor of the Age of Enlightenment* around it. Maharishi had planned a huge celebration on the lake, and all of Seelisberg was invited. It was late in the afternoon when I joined a group heading down to the dock in Treib. A glass-roofed sightseeing boat awaited us at the dock to ferry us to the center of the lake where several large steamers had been selected for the occasion. As we motored into the dark, a full moon appeared over the mountains reflecting its pearl light off the surface of the lake. Then on the horizon, a mirage of lights appeared before the white-hulled steamers came into view. They had been transformed into a floating festival of lights, strung from flagstaffs and smokestacks.

I flashed for an instant on a powerful childhood memory. It was of an experience one summer when my family rented a house on Long Island. I remembered playing on a beach with my sister watching sailboats floating at anchor. I became mesmerized by how they floated effortlessly on the surface of the water. One would think this was nothing important, but it captured me so completely that whenever my sister and I played on that beach, I'd become transfixed by the beauty of the boats at anchor. And, how they were suspended between sea and sky.

As we sidled up to the steamers, we could see how they were tied together, in a sense making one huge ship. A deckhand dropped a ladder and helped us onto the deck of one of the boats, the one reserved for the women. Heading for the boat in the center, I hurried through the salon as a flurry of women aglow in gold-trimmed saris were taking their seats.

The steamer reserved for Maharishi and his special guests was resplendent with garlands of flowers hung from the ceiling. Bright video lights were turned on in anticipation of Maharishi's arrival. His dais was set up at the forward end with his couch swathed in gold silk nestled in a multi-colored cocoon of flowers. Members of the video crew were busy focusing and color-correcting cameras.

The salon vibrated with anticipation. My 35 mm camera was the ticket that secured me a place at Maharishi's feet. Late arrivals, ferried in by smaller boats, were still arriving. Everyone had been kept guessing about what the design staff already knew: Maharishi was about to announce that the world was waking up to an era of bliss for everyone.

When the salon was full, those without seats filled the aisles and spilled out onto the deck. Maharishi walked in and made his way to the stage, stopping to greet his guests along the way. He handed Nandkishore his armful of flowers and settled onto the couch. On cue, the three ships fired up their engines and steamed farther into the infinite deepest blue of the lake.

Maharishi spoke excitedly. This was the moment in time, he said, to create an Enlightened Age, even now during Kali Yuga, the darkest cycle of time for the planet. He proclaimed that this was possible now because the growing number of meditators around the world was enlivening the expanding field of Pure Consciousness.

The room, now stuffed wall to wall with people, began to warm up. With the lack of ventilation and the heat from the video lights, the room became tropically hot. The temperature, together with the soothing cadence of Maharishi's voice, put me in a hypnotic state. An invisible stranger tugged me by the arm and pulled me out the door. I stood at the rail, refreshed by the cool night air, and found myself drifting above the steamer, above the lake, above the planet, into space. I flew past the moon and Venus, the rings of Jupiter, and the other planets until I was out of the solar system and into deep space. I marveled at the vastness of our galaxy. Farther and farther, I flew, past the Milky Way into an infinite and timeless trip until—

Until I heard a murmur coming from planet Earth.

I thought the sound seemed familiar.

Then I recognized the voice. It was the voice that had spoken to me the night I met Maharishi in the dark. It was indeed his voice.

When I looked around, I hadn't left the room at all. Someone had opened the windows and let the brisk air in. When I opened my eyes, I saw Maharishi bouncing up and down on his couch. He was laughing uncontrollably.

—At me! Always in tune with my state of mind, he was enjoying the vision that swept me away. And his laugh held the fondness I knew he had for me.

By the time I realized where I was and what was going on, Maharishi had moved on to something else. I pushed myself off the floor and made my way through the crowd and out the door, this time, for real. From on the deck, I peered back in through the window. A tall woman with long brown hair, wearing a white sari with golden trim, sat at Maharishi's feet, tuning a guitar.

I walked to the rear of the steamer and stopped at the rail to breathe in the evening air. All across the lake, the propeller-swirled water, glowing from the ships' lights, turned gold.

The swirling waters reflected the way the cosmos works with everything always in motion. Like particles in an atom, spinning around the nucleus, everything is swirling constantly, creating life out of Consciousness itself. All creation can be seen as a flowing stream of gold light. The swirling water stretched out across the surface of the lake and then into the sky. I watched the three ships, with all the people inside, leaving Planet Earth beginning a journey through infinite space. There were angels and devas and imposing gods urging them higher, and deeper into the heavenly realms.

I looked back inside to where the woman with the guitar began to sing. Her sweet voice wafted through the open windows and out the door. Her song filled the angels with delight and lifted the spirits of the gods. They all joined in. Soon the entire cosmos was singing along. When her song ended, a resounding cheer burst forth from the hearts of the audience inside, and applause reverberated among the deities above.

Maharishi was exuberant and so was everyone around him. Proclamations were being read: The Age of Enlightenment had finally dawned. Gifts were being passed out to the guests. Swiss alphorn players were called upon to blow their horns in a grand finale. The vibrant notes reflected off the lake and echoed between the mountains. The mountains played the notes back, as lively as they had been received.

Again, I felt myself floating, flying high enough to take it all in. The three steamers were skimming along on a lake as dark as the sky. Reflections of the moon and stars merged with the surface until there was no difference between the lake and the sky. The ships glided in the nothingness of space, drawing three gold lines on the Infinite Itself. Then everything became as placid as the surfaceless surface of the lake. Time didn't exist. Everything was Eternal Flow and all the angels were celebrating in Heaven and on Earth. It really *was* The Dawn of the Age of Enlightenment.

Floating somewhere above the lake and the mountains, I watched the steamers being carried along by God in a funnel of light. As they passed close by me, I saw the Swiss captain of the steamer standing at the wheel, dressed in his perfectly pressed uniform stroking his long white beard. On his face was a joy-filled smile. In his eye, a look of amazement.

Jai Guru Dev

Acknowledgements

On the level of the Relative, when I told my friend Aracely Kriete that I was inspired to write a book but didn't know about what, she immediately answered, "write about Maharishi—he's all you talk about." Her suggestion filled me with joy and, more importantly ideas, as stories of my beloved teacher came to me in bits and pieces over the next few years.

Soon after, my friend Jane Resnick, a fellow meditator and spectacularly talented editor, joined me and worked with me through the entire editing process. Jane attuned to my thought process, infused it with her own genius, making the story a true collaboration of two minds and two hearts. Most certainly, A Joy-Filled Amazement is as much Jane's as it is mine.

The title for the book is taken from The Shiva Sutras, revealed by Swami Laksmanjoo, a close friend of Maharishi's. In Verse 12, he explains the signs by which we can determine that a yogi is established in that supreme state of Lord Siva: "The predominant sign of such a yogi is joy-filled amazement."

I want to thank all the souls that shared my journey with me while in Maharishi's darshan. You, are the heart and soul of my story. You give it human breath and human attributes. I hope I have done you justice.

My hope is that my simple tale will inspire others to delve deeper into life and take their own journey through the regular practice of Maharishi's Transcendental Meditation that gives us unbounded joy from the experience of Pure Consciousness found within us all.

Certified TM teachers can be found anywhere in the world and online at: TM.org

Jai Guru Dev
Tony Anthony

Tony Anthony, Biography

 ony Anthony was born in New York and has been a writer, photojournalist, and artist. He was educated at Syracuse University and Silvermine College of Art. He served as a combat correspondent for the 198th Infantry Brigade in Vietnam in 1968 and 1969 where his stories and photographs appeared in Stars & Stripes as well as publications around the world. He was promoted to sergeant and won several medals including the Bronze Star for his reporting.

Following his tour in the Army, he began a spiritual journey working for Maharishi Mahesh Yogi for eight years as a graphic designer. He subsequently worked in New York City as a creative director until founding his own design business in Westport, Connecticut. He continued to paint and was represented by a major gallery in New York where his art was recognized by Hilton Kramer, Art Critic of the New York Times, as "distinguished for its energy, audacity and uninhibited expressionism.

Leaving the commercial world, he volunteered as a photographer for the NGO AmeriCares where his first assignment was to photograph the emergency rescue effort at the World Trade Center on 9/11. He went on to photograph the initial bombing of Baghdad at the start of the war in Iraq and an attempted coup of the government in Madagascar. He has worked on all eight continents including Antarctica where he produced a series of photos of melting glaciers.

Tony Anthony is the author of three previous books and has directed a documentary film, "Fearless Mountain" about a Buddhist forest monastery.

He resides in Northern California and has two adult sons— Evan and Andrew.

Made in the USA
Columbia, SC
20 February 2022

56536383R00173